This Dailygreatness Journal belongs to:

....

On this day of ...., I commit to practising the 8 daily steps and consciously creating a magical life of meaning, purpose and inspiration!

Signed:

....

Dailygreatness Journal: A Practical Guide For Consciously Creating Your Days
Lyndelle Palmer-Clarke

Visit Lyndelle's website at lyndellepalmerclarke.com

Help us spread our transformational journals with your friends by sharing your journal images using #dailygreatnessjournal on social media or review the Dailygreatness Journal on our website or on Amazon and go in our monthly draw to win a free copy!

To reorder your Dailygreatness Journal and browse all our other journals, online courses and content, visit dailygreatnessjournal.com

Dreaming Room Publishing
First Edition Dreaming Room 2012
Second Edition Dreaming Room 2013
Third Edition Dreaing Room 2016

Design: Viktoriya Nesheva
Printed in PRC

Copyright © 2010-2017 Dreaming Room Enterprises, AB.
All rights reserved, including the right of reproduction in whole or in part in any form.
Results may vary from person to person as with any personal development program. No express or implied guarantees are made for your personal results through using the dailygreatness journal or purchasing this product from Dreaming Room Enterprises AB.

Caution! This journal if used everyday, could radically transform, profoundly shape and dynamically alter your destiny.

Where your attention goes, energy flows. What you choose to focus on in life is magnified.

Greatness is a state of mind and cultivating that state takes daily practice. There's no magic pill for personal growth; it happens as a result of diligent, consistent inner work, and from building a solid foundation for your life to expand upon. There are millions of self-help books, coaches and courses out there but only when we apply that knowledge to our life in a practical way, can we expect to see results.

The Dailygreatness Journals were born out of frustration for how challenging it was to create lasting change in my own life. I had all the knowledge in my head from the hundreds of self-help books I'd read, but they were all just concepts. One morning, sitting on my yoga mat, I realised that the critical missing piece of the self-improvement puzzle was *applied knowledge*. Like many others also struggling to create lasting change, it wasn't a lack of willingness or knowledge that was holding me back; I was missing a structured way to apply all those self-help ideas into my life in a consistent, fun and practical way. Reading a book and putting it back on the shelf was not enough, I needed to apply those ideas and change my thinking if I was ever going to see results. It seems obvious now but at that time, there was nothing out there to help people do that. So I made it my mission to create a series of journals and planners that were a synthesis of, what I considered to be, the best personal development tools distilled down into a simple daily, weekly, quarterly and yearly format for creating lasting change.

Years later thousands of people all over the world have experienced the transformative power of the Dailygreatness Journals. My wish for you is that you also experience the same transformation that myself and others have experienced and to radically upgrade the quality of your life through this simple daily practice.

The tools in the Dailygreatness Journal help you to create change from the inside out through self-awareness, self-love, self-honesty and self-belief while tapping into your intuition and creativity. The questions and prompts lead you on a journey of self-discovery, helping you to reveal, clarify, and action your true desires. You'll learn to recognise what's holding you back, become empowered to be more creative and productive, and begin to live with more passion and purpose. Bringing together your highest ideals with your everyday life is the true essence of greatness. Give yourself time each morning and evening to becoming present, focused and conscious of your choices. This practice is not only the greatest gift you can give yourself and the people you love but it's also the path to living the life of your dreams.

I dedicate this journal to *you*, for believing in the beauty and the awesomeness of your dreams. Go and make it happen and above all, enjoy the journey!

Lyndelle Palmer-Clarke

Creating Your Perfect Life

Let's be honest; a perfect life doesn't exist but a life that is *perfect for you* is. The exciting news is, you have the power to upgrade the quality of your life, and the world around you. The problem is, most people wish for a better life and to live in a better world but they're not willing to do what it takes to get there. Your ideal life and a better world begins with a better you.

Each one of us is creating the world we live in, with every thought, every word, and every action we take. Our reality is completely of our own making, based on the perceptions and filters through which we view life. It's difficult to admit that we've created all the good and all the bad in our lives but taking responsibility for ourselves and how we show up in the world is how we grow and consiously create the world we live in.

What does your current reality look like? Is it time for an upgrade? What kind of world are you contributing to? Are you contributing at all?

Think Big, Start Small

All life upgrades start with a decision, the decision to awaken to your potential. A decision to live boldly and courageously and to finally leave your comfort zone. A decision from your heart is a force to be reckoned with and that force is the power you need to move you in the direction of your dreams. The Dailygreatness Journal will take you on a journey and help you to consolidate where you are now and where you want to go, to recognise your past achievements, identify your values, awaken to your purpose and believe in your dreams. Creating inspiring goals and a vision worth aiming for is crucial.

You'll be prompted to go within to find out what you truly desire, to uncover your *why* and decide what meaning you want your life to have.

Everything is always created twice: first in your imagination, and then in reality. When creating your overall life vision you need to think big so you don't limit yourself but remember that all achievement starts with a decision to take action.

Rituals, Habits And Magic

Forming a new habit, takes time. To successfully integrate a new habit, it's vital to create a daily ritual until your new routine becomes second nature. Working with your journal at the same time every day will help you develop a good daily routine. Give yourself the best chance by putting your Dailygreatness Journal by your bed or somewhere that you'll see it easily. Keeping it close by will help you to stay committed to the process. Don't put it on the bookshelf where you will forget about it! Magic happens when you stay committed and focused.

You'll notice I use the word 'upgrade' throughout the journal instead of words like 'fix', 'improve', or 'change'. The idea is that we don't need to 'fix' anything. Rather than thinking you need to fix yourself, personal growth is about revealing your true self and letting go of what no longer serves you. We're all on an upward spiral towards becoming a more evolved version of our former self: peeling back layers of conditioning and self-imposed limitations along the way. From now on, let's agree to use the word 'upgrade' when we talk about changing or improving anything.

The Secret to Growth

More than anything else, our outcomes and results in life are determined by our daily habits. Your mindset and how you choose to use and focus your mind is also a habit and is the single most important factor when it comes to goal achievement. Being congruent in how you think, speak, and act, lines you up for achieving your goals. Trying to achieve something without the right mindset is a waste of time and energy, and won't bring you the results you desire. The secret is to shift your focus from what you don't want, to what you do want. Becoming aware of limiting beliefs and thought patterns and how they've held you back, is one of the most profound realisations you can have. Self-knowledge is power and applying that knowledge through actively working on your mindset is the fuel that ignites your dreams.

Keeping Your Promises

Commitment is everything when it comes to unlocking your greatness. Everything you need is already inside of you and this process, if you commit to it, is the key to unlocking it. Keeping promises to yourself builds your self-esteem and confidence. If you struggle to keep small promises to yourself, then it will be difficult to reach your bigger goals. Commit to your dreams, take action and use the steps in this journal as your foundation for creating a life of greatness.

Take Action: Write a letter to your future self clearly describing what you want to achieve within the next year. Go and write it now, seal it in an envelope, write the date on the outside and mark your diary to read it in one year's time. At the end of the year, once you've completed your journal, you'll read the letter again to see how much you've grown and what you've accomplished. You'll be amazed at the result!

What's Your Dharma?

Consider the idea that we all have an inner, and an outer, purpose. Each one of us has a calling based on our unique talents and gifts. Our inner purpose is to grow, evolve, and come to know our true potential. Our outer purpose is to use our personality to do our soul's work. Simply put, your life purpose is to enrich the world through your unique gifts. When you do what you love, and love what you do, while at the same time serving others, you're fulfilling your highest purpose. In Eastern Philosophy, this is called 'dharma' – meaning your essential function or purpose in life. Consider this when it comes time to writing *Your Why* and *Personal Mission Statement*.

Getting Lost

It's easy to start strong on an exciting new adventure, but harder to stay inspired after the excitement wears off. You'll probably hit a few dips and bumps, and even miss a few days here and there, so be prepared for some backsliding. If you do, don't get down on yourself. Just acknowledge it and ask yourself some self-awareness questions to get yourself back on track. Use your answers to empower yourself, and recommit to your vision. Here are some suggestions:

What knocked me off track? Am I still inspired by my goals? What fears are holding me back? What am I choosing to focus on? What do I really desire, and what am I willing to do to get there?

The Journey

The tools in the Dailygreatness Journal are designed to slow you down so you can hear what your intuition is telling you while opening you up to new ways of thinking and being. This process may be unlike anything you've done in the past, but all transformations happen when we are willing to try new things and upgrade our behaviour. Becoming aware of our limiting beliefs, unconsious patterns and unhealthy habits and how they've held you back, is one of the most profound realisations you can have.

Life Clarity Worksheets

Soon you'll be carefully considering your deepest desires and inner longings and getting clear on your goals and what you want out of life. The Life Clarity Worksheets come with inspiration and prompts for how to get started. During this process it's important to tune into what your authentic self truly wants, so take some time to go within and contemplate your answers before completing each worksheet.

Your Why & Mission Statements

Your *Why Statement* is a clear, concise paragraph summing up your purpose, and the reason you do what you do. It should inspire and motivate you to reach for your potential each day of your life, and be the driving force behind your decisions and actions. An example of a Why Statement would be: *To awaken to my potential and help others awaken to theirs.*

Your *Personal Mission Statement* is a paragraph that clearly states how you will achieve your purpose. It can include qualities and values that you will embody and what your life, work and contribution will be about.

An example of a Personal Mission Statement might be: *Through my unique gifts and talents as a teacher, I help others develop their talent and realise their potential.*

Of course, it could be much simpler, or more complex, than this. Both your *Your Why and Personal Mission Statements* will change and evolve as you do, so don't worry too much about getting it perfect right away. Instead, think of it as fluid and changing. As you read and review your statements on a regular basis, you'll find yourself naturally embodying the thoughts and behaviours of your future self and as you become increasingly like your ideal self, you will natualy begin to bring your message and purpose into the world.

The Life Revolution

The Life Revolution tool is designed to help you get clear on how you feel about the different areas of your life. It identifies where you are happy, and areas that you'd like to upgrade. Once you've identified where you currently are in each area of your life, you can begin to make a plan to move you from where you are now to where you want to be. For full instructions for how to use The Life Revolution, see appendix iii.

Your Greatness Blueprint

After carefully considering your deepest desires, inner longings, and authentic values, you'll then move on to creating your Greatness Blueprint; a comprehensive 6-step goal planner designed for massive goal achievement. Your Blueprint is your compass and the inner vision you have for your life and is a powerful tool for goal achievement.

Take as much time as you need to complete it fully using the prompts for inspiration. If there is one worksheet you should not skip, it is this one. While it can be a little challenging to complete, it is well worth it and will serve as your roadmap for your entire next year. Once you've created a clear vision for your life, and mapped it out on your Greatness Blueprint, you'll then break it down into bite-size actions that you'll complete each day, week and quarter. A great idea is to put together a vision board that represents your Greatness Blueprint and that serves as a beautiful visual reminder to keep you inspired and on track.

The Daily Pages

The gift of a morning and evening practice has the potential to create huge shifts in the quality of your days. The Daily Pages, divided between a morning and evening session, are intended to be short, focused sessions for aligning you with your intentions and goals, to train your mind to focus on positive thoughts and to prepare you for maximum effectiveness.

How you use your journal, or how much time you spend on it each day is entirely up to you. In the beginning, you may want to start slowly by incorporating a new step every few days until you get used to the routine of all eight steps. I recommend a minimum of 30 minutes for the morning session, plus your daily exercise, and a minimum of 15 minutes for your *evening power questions*. Following this morning and evening framework is ideal, however, you can refer to your journal anytime you need inspiration, a boost to your spirit, or when you want to move into a better emotional state.

Check-Ins & Planners

Every Sunday, during your Weekly Check-In, you'll have the opportunity to look back over your week and review what is and isn't working.

Every Sunday you will also have an opportunity to plan your coming week to get a clear view of your goals, projects, and actions using the Weekly Planner. This is also a good time to review your Greatness Blueprint, Your Why Statement, and your goals to keep yourself moving towards them.

Every 90 days, you'll check in for your 90 Day Check-in to follow up on your progress, and celebrate your successes. You'll be prompted to ask yourself a series of questions designed to help you celebrate your achievements, identify areas that you'd like to upgrade and focus on ways to bring your life into balance.

After reviewing the previous quarter, and pulling into focus your most important projects and goals, you'll then plan the next quarter's goals using the 90-Day Planner.

Each weekly and quarterly review are designed to help you highlight areas that need attention and support you in upgrading those areas using your newly empowered thoughts, habits and actions while creating exciting new goals for the next quarter.

Yearly Review

At the end of the year, you will have a Yearly Review, giving you a chance to reflect on, and celebrate your achievements, learn from your challenges, and consolidate your progress, before launching into another year of greatness.

Self-Mastery & The Darkside

Self-awareness is your entry point to emotional mastery and lasting growth. The tools and self-awareness questions throughout the journal are designed to help you uncover your fears, upgrade your beliefs, and shift you into a more conscious way of life. However, focusing only on the positive and failing to recognise and acknowledge your fears, limiting beliefs, and undeveloped parts of your personality, limits your ability to achieve your potential and realise your dreams.

Self-mastery and attainment of your goals go hand-in-hand. When we don't acknowledge these undeveloped aspects of ourselves, they lie hidden in our subconscious mind and end up sabotaging even our best efforts. It takes persistent and committed work to access our unconscious, otherwise known as our 'dark-side', and to use it as a stepping stone into a better life, free from fear, reactivity, and limiting beliefs. Depending on how much you let go to the process or how willing you are to take on new concepts and ideas, you may feel wonderful while other times you may feel downright uncomfortable. This is normal. Trust that you will make progress when you commit to the process.

Your Support Crew

Once you've made the decision to live your life on purpose, it's important to find a support crew that supports you. Surrounding yourself with people who inspire and encourage you is critical. Your environment and the external influences in your life play a huge role in your ability to reach your potential. If you're not currently surrounding yourself with people who have similar hopes, dreams, goals and values as you, then find people who do. In short, hang out with and learn from those who inspire you, empower you and uplift you.

Inspiration And Motivation

One of the coolest things about this process is looking back and seeing your progress and how far you've come. Each time you do a weekly or quarterly review, you'll naturally feel inspired to continue and see how much more you can achieve. Noticing your progress gives you the confidence and motivation to overcome whatever has held you back in the past. Even the smallest of upgrades can create huge shifts in your everyday life and it's these small shifts that keep you on track and give you the ability to overcome any challenge that comes your way.

The Work

Although the journal is filled with useful planners to help you prepare and take action, it's important not to forget about your inner work. Resist using the journal solely as a diary or planner, as all eight steps are essential for living a well-balanced life and creating a successful, and purposeful year.

Words of encouragement: If all these instructions seem a little overwhelming, don't fret, soon it will all make perfect sense. Whatever you do, don't get stuck in the beginning. Do as much or as little of the clarity worksheets as you can, but don't get stuck there. Your biggest breakthroughs will happen by using the journal daily and if you're struggling to come up with your goals straight away, skip it and come back to them later when you're inspired by some worthy and meaningful goal that feels good. Relax into the process and remember to enjoy the journey.

Becoming a whole, congruent person, means the person you are on the inside, matches who you are on the out-side...

Knowing is not enough, we must apply. Willing is not enough, we must do.

Goethe

The 8 Daily Steps ›
Your foundation to a life of greatness

It's About Following Your Bliss!

1. Meditation & Visualisation

Practising meditation in the morning is a powerful way to connect with your higher self and open you to your gifts of intuition and creativity. Passive meditation quiets the mind through conscious breathing and stillness and allows you to become relaxed, centred, and present. Begin with just 5, 10 or 15 minutes twice a day and over time; you'll be able to sit for longer periods. See Appendix i for detailed instructions on basic meditation technique. Active meditation uses your imagination to consciously create your life through the use of visualisation. Tune into your inner vision and visualise on the screen of your mind what you wish to create, in as much detail as possible. Emotionally connecting to your vision through appreciation and gratitude puts you in a state of receiving, allowing your vision to happen faster. Use the power of your imagination to create your perfect day, or to focus on a goal you want to achieve. You don't always need to know exactly how it will happen; you just need to know what you want. Be prepared to take massive action and then allow the rest to unfold in perfect timing. Remember, delay is not denial, it is simply that big dreams sometimes take longer to manifest. Try the 5-step visualisation process outlined in Appendix ii.

2. Gratitude

Gratitude is a powerful emotion that opens you up to being in flow with the universe. Start your day in a state of gratitude, and allow your day to unfold from this space. Write down, using the daily gratitude list, all that you are grateful for each day. It may be as simple as the clothes you're wearing, the warm sun on your skin, or a friendship you treasure. Be grateful for things that are still coming, like new possibilities, opportunities, and connections. Whatever you focus on, you will attract more of.

3. Inspired Actions

Inspired action simply means something that you are inspired to do. It is the means to release your true genius and live with vitality and flow. When your actions are inspired, they have power and focus. With inspiration, your resistance is less and your actions become almost effortless. Instead of doing what you 'have to do,' inspired actions are things you 'love to do.' It could be a creative project, an income producing activity or anything you feel passionate about. It's about following your bliss! Choose your top three inspired actions for each day and no matter whatever happens, these are your #1 priorities to complete during that day. After you've meditated, take some time to ask questions about the best actions to take that day and contemplate what comes up. The inspirational Leonardo Da Vinci believed that quiet contemplation was the door to his genius. Try asking, "What's the best course of action to take today?" "What do I need to know today?" "What would I love to do today?" As you journal your answers and open up to your inner guidance, be alert to hunches, ideas and synchronicities that show up and guide you in certain directions, or give you flashes of inspiration and insight. When you clearly know what you want and why you want it, the inspiration will be there to guide you.

4. Intentions

Intention is your point of focus, your mindset, and what you intend to be, do, or have, at any given moment. Intention is your underlying motivation for any action you take and more than anything else, is responsible for the results you get in life. Consciously choosing your intentions, directs your focus and energy and helps you to stay centred and grounded, no matter what is happening around you. By taking responsibility for your actions and consciously choosing your emotional state, you can then respond to the world around you instead of unconsciously reacting to it. An intention can be a word, a personal value, or an affirmation starting with 'I AM' that reminds and guides you towards your highest truth. It's important to feel your intention throughout your body, as you say it aloud. Feeling your intention anchors the energy into your body's cellular memory. Stating your intentions aligns your head and your heart, and declares to yourself how you intend to co-create your life. Stating your intentions in this way creates a powerful platform from which to launch your day from. Choose your intentions carefully, as they will become your reality.

5. Dreams

Increasing your self-awareness also means becoming conscious of your dreams. If you have trouble remembering your dreams, simply start by writing down what you do remember, even if it's just a feeling. The more you do this, the more you'll remember. You can then use your dreams, their messages and their wisdom to live more consciously in your daily life. You could also use this space to journal creative ideas, your meal or exercise plan or anything that comes up during your day. If you need more space for recording your dreams, ideas, and inspirations, you might want to use a separate blank journal.

6. Inspiration

Staying inspired each day is not always easy but it's essential for keeping your inner fire lit and moving you towards your goals. Each day spend time actively working on your inspiration by reading a book or quote that inspires you, revising and reading through your goals, reading your purpose statement out loud, or listening to music or a podcast that uplifts you. Being inspired and in a positive state of mind opens you up to greater possibilities for your life.

7. Energy

High energy and vitality is a result of training your body, eating a healthy diet and focusing your mind on high energy thoughts. The more energy you have, the more productive you will be and the easier it is to achieve your goals. Energy is your most valuable resource because, when you have the energy you can see all the possibilities that are available to you. Be sure to work into your daily routine stretching, yoga, running, or any exercise that you enjoy. Feed your body healthy, nutritious foods that fuel your lifestyle and keep yourself well hydrated. The better your physiology, the better your psychology. Finally, remember to feed you mind empowering thoughts that support your goals. The combination of positive thoughts, exercise and a nutritious diet is the foundation for achieving your potential.

8. Evening Power Questions

Each night you'll have an opportunity to debrief and evaluate your day with the evening power questions. These prompts are designed to help you review your day and become more self-aware and conscious of your actions, thoughts and behaviours. Spend 15 or 20 minutes before bed to answer and contemplate these four questions. Over time notice how this simple daily practice not only clears your mind for a good night sleep but also empowers you to make more conscious choices throughout your day, making it easier to achieve your goals and make progress with your personal growth.

Self-Awareness Power Questions

Health & Body

What is one thing I can do everyday to take better care of my body?
How can I create more energy and vitality?
What do I need to STOP doing?
What do I need to START doing?
What big fitness goal will I set for myself over the next 12 months?
How can I drink more water each day?
How can I focus my diet on fresh healthy foods that bring more vitality to my life?
What does my body need right now?
What beliefs do I hold that prevent me from having the health/fitness/body I want?

Emotional, Spiritual & Personal Growth

How can I let go of limiting beliefs?
What kind of person do I aspire to be?
What are my beliefs about the nature of reality, God and why I am here?
How can I be more authentic and true to myself?
What baggage do I have that holds me back?
How is my attitude?
Am I generally positive or negative?
What stops me from having what I desire?
What do I stand for?
What fears do I have about the future?
How can I trust life more?
Who do I need to forgive?
Have I forgiven myself?
Do I listen to my heart? If not, why not?
What do I need to let go of to move forward?
What is no longer acceptable in my life?
What qualities do I wish to develop?
What is my intuition telling me about my purpose?

Intimate Relationship

What are three things that I most appreciate about my partner?
How can I bring more love into my relationship?
What are our relationship goals?
How can I be more open-minded and accepting of my partner?
What are my partners goals?
When do we have the most fun together?
Does my partner fulfill my needs and do I fulfill theirs?

Social and Fun

How can I have more fun?
What new hobby or sport would I love to start?
What do I love to do...what makes me happy?
What social club would I love to join?
What's missing in my life?
Do I have healthy fun or it is destructive?
What stops me from having more fun?
What would I love to experience just for fun?

Family and Friends

How can I give more value to those around me?
What is one thing I can do to improve my relationship with my family?
How can I listen more to those in my life?
How can I be less judgmental?
How can I expand my network and friendships?
Do I have a relationship that needs mending?
How can I surround myself with people who inspire me?
How can I be a better father/mother/sister/brother/daughter/son?
How can I be a better friend?
Who do I need to set healthy boundaries with?

Work & Career

What do I want to do with the rest of my life?
What is my definition of success?
What is my unique message and contribution?
How can I better handle obstacles and disappointments?
Am I willing to take risks to pursue my dreams?
What lies in the deepest part of my heart still to be expressed?
How can I shine my light and inspire others to shine their light?
How can I be a better leader?
What is the best and highest use of my talents?
How can I be more creative?
What new skills would I like to develop?
How can I be a better team player?
What course would I love to take?
What is my purpose in my working life?

Community and Giving

Where can I give more of my time, money or support?
How can I be a leader in my community?
What small changes can I make to my lifestyle that will positively impact the world?
What do I feel passionate about and want to support more openly?
Do I care about others?
What big community goal could I set for the next 12 months that would greatly help others?
Who could be my mentor or who could I mentor?

Money and Finances

Is making money or making a difference more important to me? Is it possible to do both?
How can I open myself to abundance and receiving more money in my life?
What decisions do I need to make that I have been putting off?
Who are my professional advisors?
What are my beliefs about money?
Which old beliefs about money, do I need to replace with new ones?
Do I believe I deserve money?
What is one idea that I have not yet acted on, that could be a successful venture?
Where and how do I sabotage my finances?
How can I get more educated on money and finances?
Do I ask enough questions around money?

Success is getting what you want; happiness is wanting what you get.

Ingrid Bergman

Forgiveness sets you free

The leaping off point begins with forgiveness. You can't successfully move forward in life and create a healthy body, mind and spirit if you're living with guilt, resentment or regret. Is there something or someone that you need to forgive to move forward with your life? It could be a person, an event, a failed business, a lost dream, a broken relationship. How about some self-forgiveness? Anything you've invested your energy in uses up your precious life force. Now's the time to forgive, let go and move on. An excellent way to do this is to write someone, or yourself, a letter that you never post. Others don't need to know that you forgive them for this to be effective. Forgiveness happens inside you. It's time now to stop holding the pain in your body, claim back your power through the act of forgiveness and free yourself up so you can go and create the life of your dreams.

My Achievements

Sometimes we need to remember how great we already are. Years go by, and we lose track of our achievements, and how much we've grown. We focus on our 'failures' and all the negative experiences overshadow our highlights. The goal here is to be completely honest with yourself and see your life with renewed perspective. Start with your childhood and do a full inventory, consolidating your life achievements to date, no matter how small they might seem now. Keep writing until you have listed them all until today. Refer to this page whenever you want to feel good about yourself, or grateful for all that life has given you. Every 90 days you will update this page with your latest and greatest achievements.

My Values

Your values in life are your own personal compass; guiding you towards what really matters to you. They are your underlying motivation for all your choices in life. Identifying your core values is one of the most profound realisations you can have. When you realise what is truly driving you and your choices, life makes a lot more sense. When your actions and your values are aligned, you are congruent and life starts to flow effortlessly. Start by identifying your core values using the list below as inspiration. Then circle your top five values that resonate with you the most. Spend time journaling below why they are important to you and how you can bring your life into alignment with your core values.

....
....
....
....
....
....
....
....
....
....
....
....
....
....
....
....

Adventure	Freedom	Independence	Security
Balance	Fulfilment	Integrity	Self-expression
Confidence	Forgiveness	Kindness	Self-reliance
Control	Fun	Knowledge	Service
Creativity	God	Love	Spirituality
Discipline	Growth	Lifestyle	Strength
Education	Happiness	Marriage	Success
Faith	Health	Peace of mind	Truth
Family	Hope	Power	Unity
Financial Security	Honesty	Progress	Wealth
Friends	Humour	Respect	Wisdom

My Dreams

Dreams are a preview of our future life. It's time now to dream big, to use your imagination to push your comfort zone and change what you believe is possible for you. Spend time answering the following questions to activate your dreams and what you would love to create over the coming year.

What do I feel passionate about? ....
....
....
....
.....................What have I always wished for in my life? ....
....
....
....
What is deep within my heart, waiting to be expressed? ....
....
....
....
...........................What would I love to be, do, or have? ....
....
....
....
............If money or time wasn't an issue, and I knew I couldn't fail, what would I do? ....
....
....
....
....
....
....
....
....

My Why

Your 'why' is your overarching goal and the reason for doing what you do. Spend time contemplating your purpose using the following questions as inspiration. What makes me come alive? What legacy do I want to leave? What gifts & talents do I wish to share with the world? What have I learnt in my life that I can pass on to others? What is my life message? What does life want from me? What wants to be expressed through me?

....
....
....
....
....
....
....
....
....
....
....
....

My Goals

Goals are your dreams with a deadline. Before creating specific goals for each area of your life, take time now to contemplate what goals are important to you, using the following questions as inspiration. What do I truly desire for my life? Why do I want it? How will I make it happen? What are the actions I need to take? When will I have it? Who do I need on my team to bring my dreams to life? For a six-step process on creating meaningful goals, see Appendix iv.

....
....
....
....
....
....
....
....
....
....
....
....

Dreams without a plan are only wishes. Dreams broken down into goals are what make dreams come true. Goals give our life meaning, a sense of purpose and fulfilment. The secret to setting goals is knowing why you want something. If you can't come up with a strong 'why', then you probably don't really want it. Your 'why' comes from within you and becomes your fuel for action. If your goals aren't congruent with your core values, you will continually sabotage yourself – or you may achieve your goals but you won't feel fulfilled. Creating goals from your heart and not your head is essential for living a fulfilling well-rounded life. We often look outside ourselves for what we think we want, but we need to consult our hearts rather than our minds to find what we truly desire for our lives. Otherwise, down the track, you may end up with a whole lot of things in your life, while missing what you're really looking for – happiness and fulfilment. Goals can be big or small, but most of all, they must be meaningful to you, or you won't have the drive to achieve them.

My Why Statement

My Personal Mission Statement

The Life Revolution

Bring the eight areas of your life into focus using The Life Revolution on the following pages, and contemplate where you are now in each area of your life by marking the circle with an **X**. Then mark where you want to be with a ✓. Write down one action that you can take immediately to move towards that goal. This will serve as a reminder of your progress as you complete another Life Revolution at each 90 Day Check-in. Transfer your actions to the Weekly and 90-Day Planners to ensure you follow through on them.

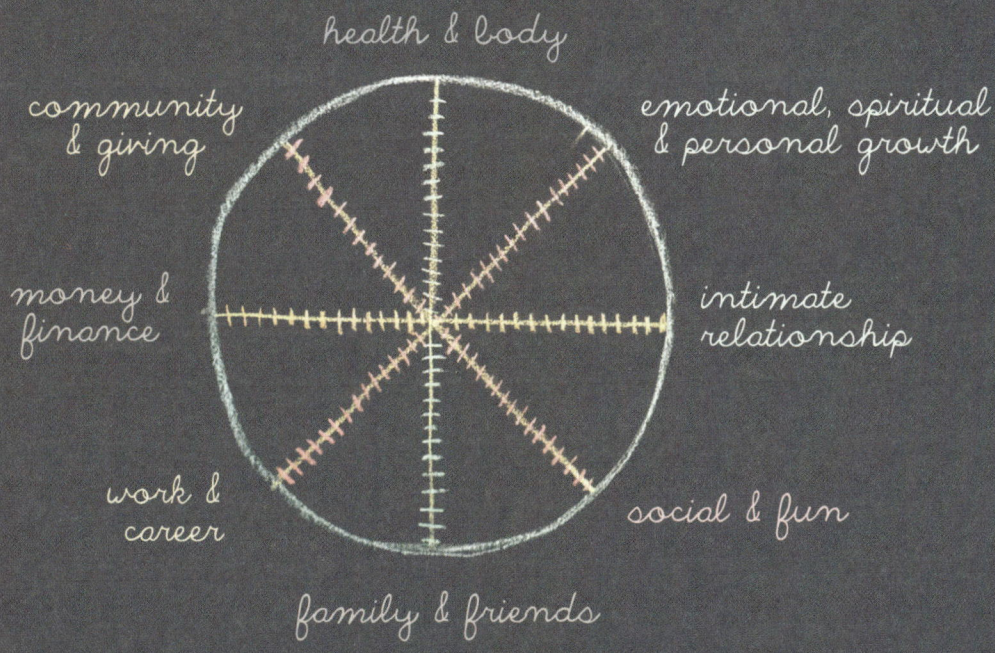

Your Life Revolution

Where I am now... · Where I want to be... · One Massive Action...

- Health & Body
- Emotional, Spiritual & Personal Growth
- Intimate Relationship
- Social & Fun
- Family & Friends
- Work & Career
- Money & Finances
- Community & Giving

Your Greatness Blueprint

WHAT is my specific goal and what do I truly want in this area of my life? What would I love to HAVE?

Add to Yearly & 90 Day Planner

WHY do I want it? What is my purpose for achieving this goal? How will this goal benefit my life or how will it affect my life, if I don't achieve it?

Use as part of your Mission & Why Statement

Area	What	Why
Health & Body		
Emotional, Spiritual & Personal Growth		
Intimate Relationship		
Social & Fun		
Family & Friends		
Work & Career		
Money & Finances		
Community & Giving		

The most difficult thing is the decision to act, the rest is merely tenacity. The fears are paper tigers. You can do anything you decide to do.

Amelia Earhart

WHEN will I achieve it?
This is my timeframe for making it happen.

Add to Yearly Planner

WHICH barriers/fears/limitations do I need to overcome to achieve this goal?

Carries over to Weekly Planner & Weekly Check-in questions.

WHO do I need to BE to achieve this goal? What mindset do I need to succeed?

What is my specific plan and what do I need to DO to make this goal happen?

These are your I AM statements

Add to 90 Day Planner, Weekly Planner & Daily Pages

January ▶
week
1 ....
2 ....
3 ....
4 ....
....

February ▶
week
1 ....
2 ....
3 ....
4 ....
....

March ▶
week
1 ....
2 ....
3 ....
4 ....
....

April ▶
week
1 ....
2 ....
3 ....
4 ....
....

May ▶
week
1 ....
2 ....
3 ....
4 ....
....

June ▶
week
1 ....
2 ....
3 ....
4 ....
....

July ▶

week

1
2
3
4

August ▶

week

1
2
3
4

September ▶

week

1
2
3
4

October ▶

week

1
2
3
4

November ▶

week

1
2
3
4

December ▶

week

1
2
3
4

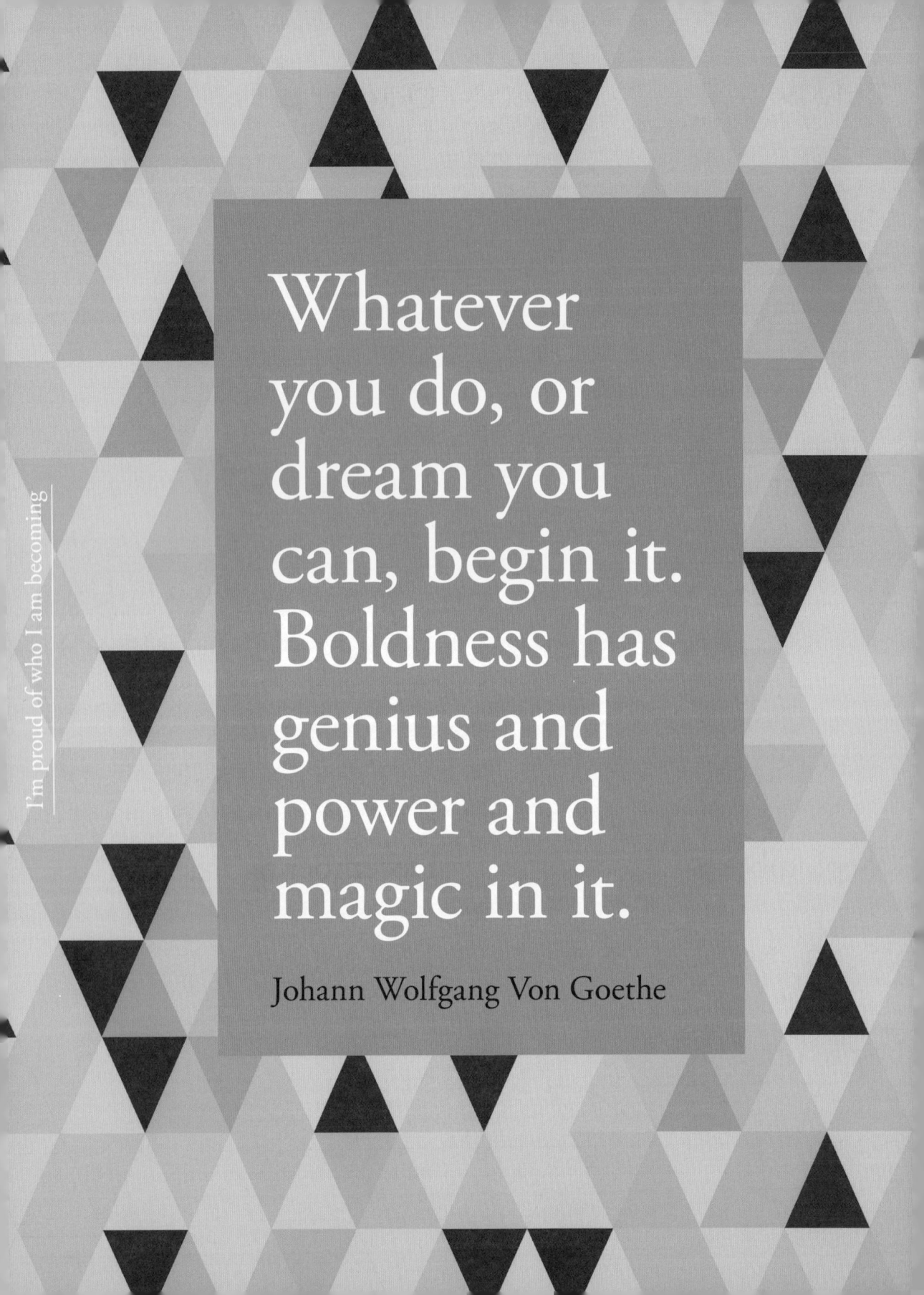

Whatever you do, or dream you can, begin it. Boldness has genius and power and magic in it.

Johann Wolfgang Von Goethe

I'm proud of who I am becoming

My goals for the next 90 days

90 Day Planner

Goal:

Project:

Target date:

Actions to complete this goal:

1.
2.
3.
4.

Why I'd love to achieve this goal:

How will I feel when I've reached this goal?

Goal:

Project:

Target date:

Actions to complete this goal:

1.
2.
3.
4.

Why I'd love to achieve this goal:

How will I feel when I've reached this goal?

Goal:

Project:

Target date:

Actions to complete this goal:

1.
2.
3.
4.

Why I'd love to achieve this goal:

How will I feel when I've reached this goal?

Goal:

Project:

Target date:

Actions to complete this goal:

1.
2.
3.
4.

Why I'd love to achieve this goal:

How will I feel when I've reached this goal?

dream space

....
....
....

Today I would love....

Today I AM so grateful for...

My top 3 inspired actions for today are...

1.
2.
3.

My intentions for today are...

I AM
I AM
I AM
I AM

What was great about today?

What did I learn today?

After today, what behaviour do I want to upgrade?

What strengths did I use today?

date:

reminders

....
....
....
....
....
....

☐ **M & V** meditation & visualisation   ☐ **I** inspiration
☐ **E** exercise

6.00
7.00
8.00
9.00
10.00
11.00
12.00
13.00
14.00
15.00
16.00
17.00
18.00
19.00
20.00

creative space

....
....
....

What if (insert possibility)....

Appreciation & Gratitude list...

☐ **M & V** ☐ **I**
meditation & visualisation   inspiration

☐ **E**   ☐ ....
exercise

Today, I AM most inspired to do these actions...

1.
2.
3.

The mindset I wish to create today is...

I AM
I AM
I AM
I AM

What did I enjoy about today?

What challenged me today that I can grow from?

What would I like to create instead?

What did I do really well today?

_____ 6.00
_____ 7.00
_____ 8.00
_____ 9.00
_____ 10.00
_____ 11.00
_____ 12.00
_____ 13.00
_____ 14.00
_____ 15.00
_____ 16.00
_____ 17.00
_____ 18.00
_____ 19.00
_____ 20.00

date:

ideas space

....
....
....

Today I accept that....

The things I AM grateful for in my life are...

Today, I would love to do these actions...

1.
2.
3.

Today I AM focusing on being...

I AM
I AM
I AM
I AM

What went well today?

What could I have handled differently today?

How can I open up to new ways of doing things?

What am I proud of about today?

date:

reminders

....
....
....
....
....
....
....

☐ **M & V** meditation & visualisation   ☐ **I** inspiration
☐ **E** exercise   ☐

I AM peaceful

6.00
7.00
8.00
9.00
10.00
11.00
12.00
13.00
14.00
15.00
16.00
17.00
18.00
19.00
20.00

thoughts space

....
....
....

Today I AM going to create...

Gratitude is Wisdom...

☐ **M & V**
    meditation & visualisation

☐ **I**
    inspiration

☐ **E**
    exercise   ....

Today, I feel inspired to do...

1.
2.
3.

Time	
6.00	
7.00	
8.00	
9.00	
10.00	
11.00	
12.00	
13.00	
14.00	
15.00	
16.00	
17.00	
18.00	
19.00	
20.00	

I create my day with my thoughts, therefore...

I AM
I AM
I AM
I AM

What did I love about today?

In what area would I like to grow?

What would I like to let go of?

How did I show leadership today?

date:

open space

....
....
....

Today I AM going to enjoy...

When I AM grateful I open up to more...

What would I do today, if it was my last?

1.
2.
3.

Today...

I AM
I AM
I AM
I AM

What was interesting about today?

What habit would I like to develop after today?

What beliefs would I like to upgrade?

What strengths did I use today?

date:

reminders

....
....
....
....
....
....
....

☐ **M & V** meditation & visualisation ☐ **I** inspiration
☐ **E** exercise ☐ ....

6.00
7.00
8.00
9.00
10.00
11.00
12.00
13.00
14.00
15.00
16.00
17.00
18.00
19.00
20.00

invention space

....
....
....

Today is my opportunity to...

Today, I give thanks for...

☐ M & V
  meditation & visualisation   ☐ I
                                  inspiration
☐ E
  exercise   ....

My inspired actions for today are...

1.
2.
3.

....	6.00
....	7.00
....	8.00
....	9.00
....	10.00
....	11.00
....	12.00
....	13.00
....	14.00
....	15.00
....	16.00
....	17.00
....	18.00
....	19.00
....	20.00

Today I honor how I feel and...

I AM
I AM
I AM
I AM

What was fun about today?

What was today's lesson?

What new behaviour can I adopt into my life?

What did I succeed at...

date:

My week in review

Weekly Check-in

What have I achieved this week?

☐ Review Greatness Blueprint

☐ Review Purpose Statement

What's working and why is it working?

☐ Update 90 Day Planner

☐ Add Actions To Weekly Planner

☐ Plan Your Week

What's not working and what am I willing to do about it?

8.00

9.00

What is one thing I can do next week that will create the biggest results in my life?

10.00

11.00

12.00

What do I need to make a decision about?

13.00

14.00

date:

15.00

Have I had fun this week? How can I have more fun?

16.00

17.00

GET SOME ALTITUDE Where is my current attitude on a scale from 1-10? How can I get some more altitude and upgrade my attitude?

18.00

19.00

What beliefs are holding me back and how can I upgrade those?

20.00

Old Habit >	New Habit >	New Actions >	New Affirmation / Mantra

My goals for the next week

Weekly Planner

My mantra for this week is ....

4 Major Goals I'm Focused On This Week

| 1. | 2. | 3. | 4. |

| Projects & appointments for this week | Target date | Actions for this week | Target date |

monday

tuesday

wednesday

thursday

friday

saturday

sunday

fun space

....
....
....

Today I AM open to the possibility of...

What I love about my work is...

Today I AM inspired to take these actions...

1.
2.
3.

I have a winning mindset and...

I AM
I AM
I AM
I AM

What have I learned today?

How was my mindset today?

What new habit do I want to adopt into my life?

How did I give value today?

date:

reminders

....
....
....
....
....
....
....

☐ **M & V** meditation & visualisation   ☐ **I** inspiration
☐ **E** exercise

6.00
7.00
8.00
9.00
10.00
11.00
12.00
13.00
14.00
15.00
16.00
17.00
18.00
19.00
20.00

genius space

....

....

....

Today, it would be fun to...

I AM present

I AM so grateful for the simple things like...

☐ M & V meditation & visualisation
☐ I inspiration
☐ E exercise
☐ ....

What is the best course of action to take today?
1.
2.
3.

6.00
7.00
8.00

Today I AM creative and...
I AM
I AM
I AM
I AM

9.00
10.00
11.00
12.00

What was fantastic about today?

13.00
14.00

What skill can I develop further?

15.00
16.00

What new mindset do I want to adopt into my life?

17.00
18.00

What did I do really well today?

19.00
20.00

date:

dream space

....
....
....

Today I would love....

Today I AM so grateful for...

My top 3 inspired actions for today are...
1.
2.
3.

My intentions for today are...
I AM
I AM
I AM
I AM

What was great about today?

What did I learn today?

After today, what behaviour do I want to upgrade?

What strengths did I use today?

date:

reminders

....
....
....
....
....
....
....
....

☐ **M & V** meditation & visualisation   ☐ **I** inspiration
☐ **E** exercise   ☐ ....

6.00
....
7.00
....
8.00
....
9.00
....
10.00
....
11.00
....
12.00
....
13.00
....
14.00
....
15.00
....
16.00
....
17.00
....
18.00
....
19.00
....
20.00
....

creative space

....
....
....

What if (insert possibility)....

Appreciation & Gratitude list...

□ **M & V** meditation & visualisation   □ **I** inspiration
□ **E** exercise

Today, I AM most inspired to do these actions...

1.
2.
3.

The mindset I wish to create today is...

I AM
I AM
I AM
I AM

What did I enjoy about today?

What challenged me today that I can grow from?

What would I like to create instead?

What did I do really well today?

6.00
7.00
8.00
9.00
10.00
11.00
12.00
13.00
14.00
15.00
16.00
17.00
18.00
19.00
20.00

date:

ideas space

....
....
....

Today I accept that....

The things I AM grateful for in my life are...

Today, I would love to do these actions...

1.
2.
3.

Today I AM focusing on being...

I AM
I AM
I AM
I AM

date:

What went well today?

What could I have handled differently today?

How can I open up to new ways of doing things?

What am I proud of about today?

reminders

....
....
....
....
....
....
....

☐ **M & V** meditation & visualisation   ☐ **I** inspiration
☐ **E** exercise   ☐ ....

6.00
7.00
8.00
9.00
10.00
11.00
12.00
13.00
14.00
15.00
16.00
17.00
18.00
19.00
20.00

thoughts space

....
....
....

....
....

Today I AM going to create...

Gratitude is Wisdom...

M & V meditation & visualisation
I inspiration
E exercise

Today, I feel inspired to do...

1.
2.
3.

6.00
7.00
8.00

I create my day with my thoughts, therefore...

9.00 I AM
      I AM
10.00 I AM
      I AM
11.00

12.00 What did I love about today?

13.00

14.00

15.00 In what area would I like to grow?

16.00

17.00 What would I like to let go of?

18.00

19.00 How did I show leadership today?

20.00

date:

My week in review

Weekly Check-in

What projects have I completed this week?

☐ Review Greatness Blueprint

☐ Review Purpose Statement

☐ Update 90 Day Planner

What's going well and why is it?

☐ Add Actions To Weekly Planner

☐ Plan Your Week

What's most challenging and how can I turn it into an opportunity?

8.00

9.00

What is one thing I can do next week that will create the biggest results in my life?

10.00

11.00

12.00

What am I happy about right now?

13.00

14.00

How am I using my time? How can I prioritise better?

15.00

16.00

17.00

GET SOME ALTITUDE Where is my current attitude on a scale from 1-10? How can I get some more altitude and upgrade my attitude?

18.00

19.00

What fears are holding me back and how can I overcome those?

20.00

date:

| Old Habit > | New Habit > | New Actions > | New Affirmation / Mantra |

My goals for the next week

Weekly Planner

My mantra for this week is
....

4 Major Goals I'm Focused On This Week

1.
2.
3.
4.

Projects & appointments for this week	Target date	Actions for this week	Target date

monday

tuesday

wednesday

thursday

friday

saturday

sunday

open space

....
....
....

Today I AM going to enjoy...

When I AM grateful I open up to more...

What would I do today, if it was my last?

1.
2.
3.

Today...

I AM
I AM
I AM
I AM

What was interesting about today?

What habit would I like to develop after today?

What beliefs would I like to upgrade?

What strengths did I use today?

date:

reminders

....
....
....
....
....
....
....

☐ **M & V** meditation & visualisation   ☐ **I** inspiration
☐ **E** exercise   ☐ ....

6.00
7.00
8.00
9.00
10.00
11.00
12.00
13.00
14.00
15.00
16.00
17.00
18.00
19.00
20.00

invention space

....
....
....

Today is my opportunity to...

Today, I give thanks for...

M & V
meditation & visualisation

I
inspiration

E
exercise

....

My inspired actions for today are...

1.
2.
3.

6.00
7.00
8.00
9.00
10.00
11.00

Today I honor how I feel and...

I AM
I AM
I AM
I AM

12.00
13.00

What was fun about today?

14.00
15.00
16.00

What was today's lesson?

17.00

What new behaviour can I adopt into my life?

18.00
19.00

What did I succeed at...

20.00

date:

fun space

....
....
....

Today I AM open to the possibility of...

What I love about my work is...

Today I AM inspired to take these actions...

1.
2.
3.

I have a winning mindset and...

I AM
I AM
I AM
I AM

What have I learned today?

How was my mindset today?

What new habit do I want to adopt into my life?

How did I give value today?

date:

reminders

....
....
....
....
....
....
....
....

☐ **M & V** meditation & visualisation   ☐ **I** inspiration
☐ **E** exercise   ☐ ....

6.00
7.00
8.00
9.00
10.00
11.00
12.00
13.00
14.00
15.00
16.00
17.00
18.00
19.00
20.00

genius space

....
....
....

Today, it would be fun to...

I AM so grateful for the simple things like...

M & V meditation & visualisation
I inspiration
E exercise

What is the best course of action to take today?

1.
2.
3.

Today I AM creative and...

I AM
I AM
I AM
I AM

	6.00
	7.00
	8.00
	9.00
	10.00
	11.00
	12.00
	13.00
	14.00
	15.00
	16.00
	17.00
	18.00
	19.00
	20.00

What was fantastic about today?

What skill can I develop further?

What new mindset do I want to adopt into my life?

What did I do really well today?

date:

dream space

....
....
....

Today I would love....

Today I AM so grateful for...

My top 3 inspired actions for today are...

1.
2.
3.

My intentions for today are...

I AM
I AM
I AM
I AM

What was great about today?

What did I learn today?

After today, what behaviour do I want to upgrade?

What strengths did I use today?

date:

reminders

....
....
....
....
....
....
....
....

☐ **M & V** meditation & visualisation   ☐ **I** inspiration
☐ **E** exercise   ☐ ....

Time	
6.00	
7.00	
8.00	
9.00	
10.00	
11.00	
12.00	
13.00	
14.00	
15.00	
16.00	
17.00	
18.00	
19.00	
20.00	

creative space

....
....
....

What if (insert possibility)....

Appreciation & Gratitude list...

Today, I AM most inspired to do these actions...

1.
2.
3.

The mindset I wish to create today is...

I AM
I AM
I AM
I AM

What did I enjoy about today?

What challenged me today that I can grow from?

What would I like to create instead?

What did I do really well today?

M & V meditation & visualisation
I inspiration
E exercise

6.00
7.00
8.00
9.00
10.00
11.00
12.00
13.00
14.00
15.00
16.00
17.00
18.00
19.00
20.00

date:

My week in review

Weekly Check-in

What have I achieved on my greatness blueprint this week?

☐ Review Greatness Blueprint

☐ Review Purpose Statement

Where am I seeing the desired results & why?

☐ Update 90 Day Planner

☐ Add Actions To Weekly Planner

☐ Plan Your Week

What do I need to start or stop?

What is one thing I can do next week that will create the biggest results in my life?

Where can I be a better leader?

Do I need to upgrade my communication skills? How can I be better?

GET SOME ALTITUDE Where is my current attitude on a scale from 1 -10? How can I get some more altitude and upgrade my attitude?

What negative attitudes are holding me back and how can I overcome those?

date:

8.00
9.00
10.00
11.00
12.00
13.00
14.00
15.00
16.00
17.00
18.00
19.00
20.00

Old Habit >	New Habit >	New Actions >	New Affirmation / Mantra

My goals for the next week

Weekly Planner

My mantra for this week is ....

4 Major Goals I'm Focused On This Week

| 1. | 2. | 3. | 4. |

| Projects & appointments for this week | Target date | Actions for this week | Target date |

- monday
- tuesday
- wednesday
- thursday
- friday
- saturday
- sunday

ideas space

....
....
....

Today I accept that....

The things I AM grateful for in my life are...

Today, I would love to do these actions...
1.
2.
3.

Today I AM focusing on being...

I AM
I AM
I AM
I AM

What went well today?

What could I have handled differently today?

How can I open up to new ways of doing things?

What am I proud of about today?

date:

reminders

....
....
....
....
....
....
....

| ☐ **M & V** meditation & visualisation | ☐ **I** inspiration |
| ☐ **E** exercise | ☐ .... |

6.00
....
7.00
....
8.00
....
9.00
....
10.00
....
11.00
....
12.00
....
13.00
....
14.00
....
15.00
....
16.00
....
17.00
....
18.00
....
19.00
....
20.00
....

thoughts space

....
....
....

....
....
....
....
....
....
....
....

Today I AM going to create...

☐ **M & V** meditation & visualisation   ☐ **I** inspiration
☐ **E** exercise   ....

Gratitude is Wisdom...

Today, I feel inspired to do...

1.
2.
3.

....	6.00
....	7.00
....	8.00
....	9.00
....	10.00
....	11.00
....	12.00
....	13.00
....	14.00
....	15.00
....	16.00
....	17.00
....	18.00
....	19.00
....	20.00

I create my day with my thoughts, therefore...

I AM
I AM
I AM
I AM

What did I love about today?

In what area would I like to grow?

What would I like to let go of?

How did I show leadership today?

date:

open space

....
....
....

Today I AM going to enjoy...

When I AM grateful I open up to more...

What would I do today, if it was my last?

1.
2.
3.

Today...

I AM
I AM
I AM
I AM

What was interesting about today?

What habit would I like to develop after today?

What beliefs would I like to upgrade?

What strengths did I use today?

date:

reminders

....
....
....
....
....
....
....

☐ **M & V** meditation & visualisation   ☐ **I** inspiration
☐ **E** exercise   ☐ ....

6.00
7.00
8.00
9.00
10.00
11.00
12.00
13.00
14.00
15.00
16.00
17.00
18.00
19.00
20.00

invention space

I AM creative

Today is my opportunity to...

Today, I give thanks for...

☐ M & V
meditation & visualisation
☐ I
inspiration
☐ E
exercise

My inspired actions for today are...

1.
2.
3.

6.00
7.00
8.00
9.00
10.00
11.00

Today I honor how I feel and...

I AM
I AM
I AM
I AM

12.00
13.00
14.00
15.00
16.00
17.00
18.00
19.00
20.00

What was fun about today?

What was today's lesson?

What new behaviour can I adopt into my life?

What did I succeed at...

date:

fun space

....
....
....

Today I AM open to the possibility of...

What I love about my work is...

Today I AM inspired to take these actions...

1.
2.
3.

I have a winning mindset and...

I AM
I AM
I AM
I AM

What have I learned today?

How was my mindset today?

What new habit do I want to adopt into my life?

How did I give value today?

date:

reminders

....
....
....
....
....
....
....

☐ **M & V** meditation & visualisation   ☐ **I** inspiration
☐ **E** exercise   ☐ ....

6.00
7.00
8.00
9.00
10.00
11.00
12.00
13.00
14.00
15.00
16.00
17.00
18.00
19.00
20.00

genius space

....
....
....

Today, it would be fun to...

I AM so grateful for the simple things like...

☐ M & V ☐ I
   meditation & visualisation   inspiration
☐ E
   exercise ☐ ....

What is the best course of action to take today?

1.
2.
3.

6.00
7.00
8.00

Today I AM creative and...

I AM
I AM
I AM
I AM

9.00
10.00
11.00
12.00

What was fantastic about today?

13.00
14.00

What skill can I develop further?

15.00
16.00
17.00

What new mindset do I want to adopt into my life?

18.00
19.00

What did I do really well today?

20.00

date:

My week in review

Weekly Check-in

What major goals have I achieved this month?

☐ Review Greatness Blueprint

☐ Review Purpose Statement

Where am I having success and why?

☐ Update 90 Day Planner

☐ Add Actions To Weekly Planner

☐ Plan Your Week

What are the biggest distractions in my life and how can I remove them?

8.00

9.00

What is one thing I can do next week that will create the biggest results in my life?

10.00

11.00

What am I committed to achieving in my life right now?

12.00

13.00

What is my home and work environment like? Does it inspire me?

14.00

15.00

16.00

GET SOME ALTITUDE Where is my current attitude on a scale from 1-10? How can I get some more altitude and upgrade my attitude?

17.00

18.00

What disempowering thoughts are holding me back and how can I upgrade those?

19.00

20.00

date:

| Old Habit > | New Habit > | New Actions > | New Affirmation / Mantra |

My goals for the next week

Weekly Planner

My mantra for this week is
....

4 Major Goals I'm Focused On This Week

1.   2.   3.   4.

Projects & appointments for this week	Target date	Actions for this week	Target date
monday			
tuesday			
wednesday			
thursday			
friday			
saturday			
sunday			

dream space

....
....
....

Today I would love....

Today I AM so grateful for...

My top 3 inspired actions for today are...

1.
2.
3.

My intentions for today are...

I AM
I AM
I AM
I AM

What was great about today?

What did I learn today?

After today, what behaviour do I want to upgrade?

What strengths did I use today?

date:

reminders

....
....
....
....
....
....
....

☐ **M & V** meditation & visualisation ☐ **I** inspiration
☐ **E** exercise ☐ ....

6.00
7.00
8.00
9.00
10.00
11.00
12.00
13.00
14.00
15.00
16.00
17.00
18.00
19.00
20.00

creative space

....
....
....

What if (insert possibility)....

Appreciation & Gratitude list...

☐ M & V meditation & visualisation
☐ E exercise
☐ I inspiration
☐ ....

Today, I AM most inspired to do these actions...

1.
2.
3.

The mindset I wish to create today is...

I AM
I AM
I AM
I AM

What did I enjoy about today?

What challenged me today that I can grow from?

What would I like to create instead?

What did I do really well today?

_____ 6.00
_____ 7.00
_____ 8.00
_____ 9.00
_____ 10.00
_____ 11.00
_____ 12.00
_____ 13.00
_____ 14.00
_____ 15.00
_____ 16.00
_____ 17.00
_____ 18.00
_____ 19.00
_____ 20.00

date:

ideas space

....

....

....

Today I accept that....

The things I AM grateful for in my life are...

Today, I would love to do these actions...

1.
2.
3.

Today I AM focusing on being...

I AM

I AM

I AM

I AM

What went well today?

What could I have handled differently today?

How can I open up to new ways of doing things?

What am I proud of about today?

date:

reminders

....

....

....

....

....

....

....

....

☐ **M & V** meditation & visualisation   ☐ **I** inspiration
☐ **E** exercise   ☐ ....

I AM peaceful

6.00
7.00
8.00
9.00
10.00
11.00
12.00
13.00
14.00
15.00
16.00
17.00
18.00
19.00
20.00

thoughts space

....

....

....

....

.... Today I AM going to create...

....

....

....

.... Gratitude is Wisdom...

....

M & V	☐	I
meditation & visualisation		inspiration
E ☐	☐	
exercise		....

Today, I feel inspired to do...

1.
2.
3.

_____ 6.00
_____
_____ 7.00
_____
_____ 8.00   I create my day with my thoughts, therefore...
_____
_____ 9.00   I AM
_____   I AM
_____ 10.00   I AM
_____   I AM
_____ 11.00
_____
_____ 12.00   What did I love about today?
_____
_____ 13.00
_____
_____ 14.00
_____
_____ 15.00   In what area would I like to grow?
_____
_____ 16.00
_____
_____ 17.00   What would I like to let go of?
_____
_____ 18.00
_____
_____ 19.00   How did I show leadership today?
_____
_____ 20.00

date:

open space

....
....
....

Today I AM going to enjoy...

When I AM grateful I open up to more...

What would I do today, if it was my last?

1.
2.
3.

Today...

I AM
I AM
I AM
I AM

What was interesting about today?

What habit would I like to develop after today?

What beliefs would I like to upgrade?

What strengths did I use today?

date:

reminders

....
....
....
....
....
....
....
....

☐ **M & V** meditation & visualisation ☐ **I** inspiration
☐ **E** exercise ☐ ....

Time	
6.00	
7.00	
8.00	
9.00	
10.00	
11.00	
12.00	
13.00	
14.00	
15.00	
16.00	
17.00	
18.00	
19.00	
20.00	

invention space

....
....
....

Today is my opportunity to...

Today, I give thanks for...

☐ **M & V** meditation & visualisation
☐ **I** inspiration
☐ **E** exercise
☐ ....

My inspired actions for today are...

1.
2.
3.

Today I honor how I feel and...

I AM
I AM
I AM
I AM

6.00
7.00
8.00
9.00
10.00
11.00
12.00 What was fun about today?
13.00
14.00
15.00 What was today's lesson?
16.00
17.00 What new behaviour can I adopt into my life?
18.00
19.00 What did I succeed at...
20.00

date:

My week in review

Weekly Check-in

What have I achieved this week?

☐ Review Greatness Blueprint

☐ Review Purpose Statement

What's working and why is it working?

☐ Update 90 Day Planner

☐ Add Actions To Weekly Planner

☐ Plan Your Week

What's not working and what am I willing to do about it?

8.00

9.00

What is one thing I can do next week that will create the biggest results in my life?

10.00

11.00

12.00

What do I need to make a decision about?

13.00

14.00

Have I had fun this week? How can I have more fun?

15.00

16.00

GET SOME ALTITUDE Where is my current attitude on a scale from 1-10? How can I get some more altitude and upgrade my attitude?

17.00

18.00

19.00

What beliefs are holding me back and how can I upgrade those?

20.00

date:

Old Habit >	New Habit >	New Actions >	New Affirmation / Mantra

My goals for the next week

Weekly Planner

My mantra for this week is ....

4 Major Goals I'm Focused On This Week

| 1. | 2. | 3. | 4. |

| Projects & appointments for this week | Target date | Actions for this week | Target date |

monday

tuesday

wednesday

thursday

friday

saturday

sunday

fun space

....
....
....

Today I AM open to the possibility of...

What I love about my work is...

Today I AM inspired to take these actions...

1.
2.
3.

I have a winning mindset and...

I AM
I AM
I AM
I AM

What have I learned today?

How was my mindset today?

What new habit do I want to adopt into my life?

How did I give value today?

date:

reminders

....
....
....
....
....
....
....

☐ **M & V** meditation & visualisation   ☐ **I** inspiration
☐ **E** exercise   ☐ ....

6.00
7.00
8.00
9.00
10.00
11.00
12.00
13.00
14.00
15.00
16.00
17.00
18.00
19.00
20.00

genius space

....
....
....

I AM present

Today, it would be fun to...

I AM so grateful for the simple things like...

M & V meditation & visualisation
I inspiration
E exercise
....

What is the best course of action to take today?

1.
2.
3.

_____	6.00
_____	7.00
_____	8.00
_____	9.00
_____	10.00
_____	11.00
_____	12.00
_____	13.00
_____	14.00
_____	15.00
_____	16.00
_____	17.00
_____	18.00
_____	19.00
_____	20.00

Today I AM creative and...

I AM
I AM
I AM
I AM

What was fantastic about today?

What skill can I develop further?

What new mindset do I want to adopt into my life?

What did I do really well today?

date:

dream space

....
....
....

Today I would love....

Today I AM so grateful for...

My top 3 inspired actions for today are...
1.
2.
3.

My intentions for today are...
I AM
I AM
I AM
I AM

What was great about today?

What did I learn today?

After today, what behaviour do I want to upgrade?

What strengths did I use today?

date:

reminders

....
....
....
....
....
....
....

☐ **M & V** meditation & visualisation ☐ **I** inspiration
☐ **E** exercise ☐ ....

6.00
7.00
8.00
9.00
10.00
11.00
12.00
13.00
14.00
15.00
16.00
17.00
18.00
19.00
20.00

creative space

....
....
....

What if (insert possibility)....

Appreciation & Gratitude list...

Today, I AM most inspired to do these actions...

1.
2.
3.

The mindset I wish to create today is...

I AM
I AM
I AM
I AM

What did I enjoy about today?

What challenged me today that I can grow from?

What would I like to create instead?

What did I do really well today?

....
....
....
....
....
....
....

M & V meditation & visualisation
I inspiration
E exercise

6.00
7.00
8.00
9.00
10.00
11.00
12.00
13.00
14.00
15.00
16.00
17.00
18.00
19.00
20.00

date:

ideas space

....
....
....

Today I accept that....

The things I AM grateful for in my life are...

Today, I would love to do these actions...

1.
2.
3.

Today I AM focusing on being...

I AM
I AM
I AM
I AM

What went well today?

What could I have handled differently today?

How can I open up to new ways of doing things?

What am I proud of about today?

date:

reminders

....
....
....
....
....
....
....

☐ **M & V** meditation & visualisation   ☐ **I** inspiration
☐ **E** exercise   ☐ ....

6.00
7.00
8.00
9.00
10.00
11.00
12.00
13.00
14.00
15.00
16.00
17.00
18.00
19.00
20.00

thoughts space

....
....
....

Today I AM going to create...

Gratitude is Wisdom...

M & V meditation & visualisation
I inspiration
E exercise

Today, I feel inspired to do...

1.
2.
3.

- 6.00
- 7.00
- 8.00
- 9.00
- 10.00
- 11.00

I create my day with my thoughts, therefore...

I AM
I AM
I AM
I AM

- 12.00
- 13.00

What did I love about today?

- 14.00
- 15.00
- 16.00

In what area would I like to grow?

- 17.00

What would I like to let go of?

- 18.00
- 19.00

How did I show leadership today?

- 20.00

date:

My week in review

Weekly Check-in

What projects have I completed this week?

☐ Review Greatness Blueprint

☐ Review Purpose Statement

☐ Update 90 Day Planner

What's going well and why is it?

☐ Add Actions To Weekly Planner

☐ Plan Your Week

What's most challenging and how can I turn it into an opportunity?

8.00

9.00

What is one thing I can do next week that will create the biggest results in my life?

10.00

11.00

12.00

What am I happy about right now?

13.00

14.00

How am I using my time? How can I prioritise better?

15.00

16.00

GET SOME ALTITUDE Where is my current attitude on a scale from 1-10? How can I get some more altitude and upgrade my attitude?

17.00

18.00

19.00

What fears are holding me back and how can I overcome those?

20.00

date:

| Old Habit > | New Habit > | New Actions > | New Affirmation / Mantra |

My goals for the next week

Weekly Planner

My mantra for this week is ....

4 Major Goals I'm Focused On This Week

| 1. | 2. | 3. | 4. |

| Projects & appointments for this week | Target date | Actions for this week | Target date |

monday

tuesday

wednesday

thursday

friday

saturday

sunday

open space

....
....
....

Today I AM going to enjoy...

When I AM grateful I open up to more...

What would I do today, if it was my last?

1.
2.
3.

Today...

I AM
I AM
I AM
I AM

What was interesting about today?

What habit would I like to develop after today?

What beliefs would I like to upgrade?

What strengths did I use today?

date:

reminders

....
....
....
....
....
....
....

☐ **M & V** meditation & visualisation ☐ **I** inspiration
☐ **E** exercise

6.00
7.00
8.00
9.00
10.00
11.00
12.00
13.00
14.00
15.00
16.00
17.00
18.00
19.00
20.00

invention space

....
....
....

Today is my opportunity to...

Today, I give thanks for...

☐ M & V   ☐ I
  meditation & visualisation   inspiration
☐ E   ☐ ....
  exercise

My inspired actions for today are...

1.
2.
3.

6.00
7.00
8.00   Today I honor how I feel and...
9.00   I AM
          I AM
10.00   I AM
          I AM
11.00
12.00   What was fun about today?
13.00
14.00
          What was today's lesson?
15.00
16.00
          What new behaviour can I adopt into my life?
17.00
18.00
19.00   What did I succeed at...
20.00

date:

fun space

....

....

....

Today I AM open to the possibility of...

What I love about my work is...

Today I AM inspired to take these actions...

1.
2.
3.

I have a winning mindset and...

I AM
I AM
I AM
I AM

What have I learned today?

How was my mindset today?

What new habit do I want to adopt into my life?

How did I give value today?

date:

reminders

....

....

....

....

....

....

....

☐ **M & V** meditation & visualisation   ☐ **I** inspiration

☐ **E** exercise   ☐ ....

6.00
7.00
8.00
9.00
10.00
11.00
12.00
13.00
14.00
15.00
16.00
17.00
18.00
19.00
20.00

genius space

....
....
....
....
....
....

Today, it would be fun to...

I AM so grateful for the simple things like...

M & V — meditation & visualisation
I — inspiration
E — exercise

What is the best course of action to take today?

1.
2.
3.

6.00
7.00
8.00

Today I AM creative and...

I AM
I AM
I AM
I AM

9.00
10.00
11.00
12.00

What was fantastic about today?

13.00
14.00

What skill can I develop further?

15.00
16.00

What new mindset do I want to adopt into my life?

17.00
18.00

What did I do really well today?

19.00
20.00

date:

dream space

....
....
....

Today I would love....

Today I AM so grateful for...

My top 3 inspired actions for today are...

1.
2.
3.

My intentions for today are...

I AM
I AM
I AM
I AM

What was great about today?

What did I learn today?

After today, what behaviour do I want to upgrade?

What strengths did I use today?

date:

reminders

....
....
....
....
....
....

☐ **M & V** meditation & visualisation   ☐ **I** inspiration
☐ **E** exercise   ☐ ....

6.00
7.00
8.00
9.00
10.00
11.00
12.00
13.00
14.00
15.00
16.00
17.00
18.00
19.00
20.00

creative space

....
....
....

What if (insert possibility)....

....
....
....

Appreciation & Gratitude list...

☐ M & V
   meditation & visualisation
☐ I
   inspiration
☐ E
   exercise
☐ ....

Today, I AM most inspired to do these actions...
1.
2.
3.

The mindset I wish to create today is...
I AM
I AM
I AM
I AM

6.00
7.00
8.00
9.00
10.00
11.00
12.00   What did I enjoy about today?
13.00
14.00
15.00   What challenged me today that I can grow from?
16.00
17.00   What would I like to create instead?
18.00
19.00   What did I do really well today?
20.00

date:

My week in review

Weekly Check-in

What have I achieved on my greatness blueprint this week?

☐ Review Greatness Blueprint

☐ Review Purpose Statement

Where am I seeing the desired results & why?

☐ Update 90 Day Planner

☐ Add Actions To Weekly Planner

☐ Plan Your Week

What do I need to start or stop?

8.00

9.00

What is one thing I can do next week that will create the biggest results in my life?

10.00

11.00

12.00

Where can I be a better leader?

13.00

14.00

date:

Do I need to upgrade my communication skills? How can I be better?

15.00

16.00

GET SOME ALTITUDE Where is my current attitude on a scale from 1-10? How can I get some more altitude and upgrade my attitude?

17.00

18.00

19.00

What negative attitudes are holding me back and how can I overcome those?

20.00

| Old Habit > | New Habit > | New Actions > | New Affirmation / Mantra |

My goals for the next week

Weekly Planner

My mantra for this week is ....

4 Major Goals I'm Focused On This Week

| 1. | 2. | 3. | 4. |

| Projects & appointments for this week | Target date | Actions for this week | Target date |

monday

tuesday

wednesday

thursday

friday

saturday

sunday

ideas space

....
....
....

Today I accept that....

The things I AM grateful for in my life are...

Today, I would love to do these actions...

1.
2.
3.

Today I AM focusing on being...

I AM
I AM
I AM
I AM

What went well today?

What could I have handled differently today?

How can I open up to new ways of doing things?

What am I proud of about today?

date:

reminders

....
....
....
....
....
....
....

☐ **M & V** meditation & visualisation   ☐ **I** inspiration
☐ **E** exercise   ☐ ....

6.00
7.00
8.00
9.00
10.00
11.00
12.00
13.00
14.00
15.00
16.00
17.00
18.00
19.00
20.00

thoughts space

....
....
....

Today I AM going to create...

Gratitude is Wisdom...

☐ M & V
  meditation & visualisation   ☐ I
                                   inspiration
☐ E
  exercise   ☐ ....

Today, I feel inspired to do...

1.
2.
3.

I create my day with my thoughts, therefore...

I AM
I AM
I AM
I AM

What did I love about today?

In what area would I like to grow?

What would I like to let go of?

How did I show leadership today?

_____ 6.00
_____ 7.00
_____ 8.00
_____ 9.00
_____ 10.00
_____ 11.00
_____ 12.00
_____ 13.00
_____ 14.00
_____ 15.00
_____ 16.00
_____ 17.00
_____ 18.00
_____ 19.00
_____ 20.00

date:

open space

....
....
....

Today I AM going to enjoy...

When I AM grateful I open up to more...

What would I do today, if it was my last?
1.
2.
3.

Today...
I AM
I AM
I AM
I AM

What was interesting about today?

What habit would I like to develop after today?

What beliefs would I like to upgrade?

What strengths did I use today?

date:

reminders

....
....
....
....
....
....
....

☐ **M & V** meditation & visualisation   ☐ **I** inspiration
☐ **E** exercise   ☐ ....

6.00
7.00
8.00
9.00
10.00
11.00
12.00
13.00
14.00
15.00
16.00
17.00
18.00
19.00
20.00

invention space

....
....
....

I AM creative

Today is my opportunity to...

Today, I give thanks for...

M & V meditation & visualisation	I inspiration
E exercise	....

My inspired actions for today are...

1.
2.
3.

6.00
7.00
8.00   Today I honor how I feel and...
9.00   I AM
         I AM
10.00   I AM
         I AM
11.00
12.00   What was fun about today?
13.00
14.00   What was today's lesson?
15.00
16.00
17.00   What new behaviour can I adopt into my life?
18.00
19.00   What did I succeed at...
20.00

date:

fun space

....
....
....

Today I AM open to the possibility of...

What I love about my work is...

Today I AM inspired to take these actions...
1.
2.
3.

I have a winning mindset and...
I AM
I AM
I AM
I AM

What have I learned today?

How was my mindset today?

What new habit do I want to adopt into my life?

How did I give value today?

date:

reminders

....
....
....
....
....
....

☐ **M & V** meditation & visualisation ☐ **I** inspiration
☐ **E** exercise ☐ ....

Time	
6.00	
7.00	
8.00	
9.00	
10.00	
11.00	
12.00	
13.00	
14.00	
15.00	
16.00	
17.00	
18.00	
19.00	
20.00	

genius space

....
....
....

Today, it would be fun to...

I AM so grateful for the simple things like...

☐ M & V
   meditation & visualisation
☐ I
   inspiration
☐ E
   exercise
☐ ....

What is the best course of action to take today?

1.
2.
3.

Today I AM creative and...

I AM
I AM
I AM
I AM

What was fantastic about today?

What skill can I develop further?

What new mindset do I want to adopt into my life?

What did I do really well today?

- 6.00
- 7.00
- 8.00
- 9.00
- 10.00
- 11.00
- 12.00
- 13.00
- 14.00
- 15.00
- 16.00
- 17.00
- 18.00
- 19.00
- 20.00

date:

My week in review

Weekly Check-in

What major goals have I achieved this month?

☐ Review Greatness Blueprint

☐ Review Purpose Statement

Where am I having success and why?

☐ Update 90 Day Planner

☐ Add Actions To Weekly Planner

☐ Plan Your Week

What are the biggest distractions in my life and how can I remove them?

8.00

9.00

What is one thing I can do next week that will create the biggest results in my life?

10.00

11.00

What am I committed to achieving in my life right now?

12.00

13.00

14.00

What is my home and work environment like? Does it inspire me?

15.00

16.00

GET SOME ALTITUDE Where is my current attitude on a scale from 1-10? How can I get some more altitude and upgrade my attitude?

17.00

18.00

19.00

What disempowering thoughts are holding me back and how can I upgrade those?

20.00

date:

| Old Habit > | New Habit > | New Actions > | New Affirmation / Mantra |

My goals for the next week

Weekly Planner

My mantra for this week is ....

4 Major Goals I'm Focused On This Week

| 1. | 2. | 3. | 4. |

| Projects & appointments for this week | Target date | Actions for this week | Target date |

monday

tuesday

wednesday

thursday

friday

saturday

sunday

dream space

....
....
....

Today I would love....

Today I AM so grateful for...

My top 3 inspired actions for today are...

1.
2.
3.

My intentions for today are...

I AM
I AM
I AM
I AM

What was great about today?

What did I learn today?

After today, what behaviour do I want to upgrade?

What strengths did I use today?

date:

reminders

....
....
....
....
....
....
....

☐ **M & V** meditation & visualisation   ☐ **I** inspiration
☐ **E** exercise   ☐ ....

6.00
7.00
8.00
9.00
10.00
11.00
12.00
13.00
14.00
15.00
16.00
17.00
18.00
19.00
20.00

creative space

....
....
....

What if (insert possibility)....

Appreciation & Gratitude list...

Today, I AM most inspired to do these actions...

1.
2.
3.

The mindset I wish to create today is...

I AM
I AM
I AM
I AM

What did I enjoy about today?

What challenged me today that I can grow from?

What would I like to create instead?

What did I do really well today?

M & V meditation & visualisation
I inspiration
E exercise

....

6.00
7.00
8.00
9.00
10.00
11.00
12.00
13.00
14.00
15.00
16.00
17.00
18.00
19.00
20.00

date:

ideas space

....
....
....

Today I accept that....

The things I AM grateful for in my life are...

Today, I would love to do these actions...

1.
2.
3.

Today I AM focusing on being...

I AM
I AM
I AM
I AM

What went well today?

What could I have handled differently today?

How can I open up to new ways of doing things?

What am I proud of about today?

date:

reminders

....
....
....
....
....
....
....
....

☐ **M & V** meditation & visualisation ☐ **I** inspiration
☐ **E** exercise ☐ ....

I AM peaceful

6.00
7.00
8.00
9.00
10.00
11.00
12.00
13.00
14.00
15.00
16.00
17.00
18.00
19.00
20.00

thoughts space

....
....
....

Today I AM going to create...

Gratitude is Wisdom...

M & V meditation & visualisation	**I** inspiration
E exercise	....

Today, I feel inspired to do...

1.
2.
3.

I create my day with my thoughts, therefore...

I AM
I AM
I AM
I AM

What did I love about today?

In what area would I like to grow?

What would I like to let go of?

How did I show leadership today?

- 6.00
- 7.00
- 8.00
- 9.00
- 10.00
- 11.00
- 12.00
- 13.00
- 14.00
- 15.00
- 16.00
- 17.00
- 18.00
- 19.00
- 20.00

date:

open space

....
....
....

Today I AM going to enjoy...

When I AM grateful I open up to more...

What would I do today, if it was my last?

1.
2.
3.

Today...

I AM
I AM
I AM
I AM

What was interesting about today?

What habit would I like to develop after today?

What beliefs would I like to upgrade?

What strengths did I use today?

date:

reminders

....
....
....
....
....
....
....

☐ **M & V** meditation & visualisation ☐ **I** inspiration
☐ **E** exercise ☐ ....

6.00
7.00
8.00
9.00
10.00
11.00
12.00
13.00
14.00
15.00
16.00
17.00
18.00
19.00
20.00

invention space

....
....
....

Today is my opportunity to...

Today, I give thanks for...

My inspired actions for today are...

1.
2.
3.

Today I honor how I feel and...

I AM
I AM
I AM
I AM

What was fun about today?

What was today's lesson?

What new behaviour can I adopt into my life?

What did I succeed at...

M & V meditation & visualisation
I inspiration
E exercise

- 6.00
- 7.00
- 8.00
- 9.00
- 10.00
- 11.00
- 12.00
- 13.00
- 14.00
- 15.00
- 16.00
- 17.00
- 18.00
- 19.00
- 20.00

date:

My week in review

Weekly Check-in

What have I achieved this week?

☐ Review Greatness Blueprint

☐ Review Purpose Statement

☐ Update 90 Day Planner

What's working and why is it working?

☐ Add Actions To Weekly Planner

☐ Plan Your Week

What's not working and what am I willing to do about it?

8.00

9.00

What is one thing I can do next week that will create the biggest results in my life?

10.00

11.00

What do I need to make a decision about?

12.00

13.00

14.00

Have I had fun this week? How can I have more fun?

15.00

16.00

GET SOME ALTITUDE Where is my current attitude on a scale from 1-10? How can I get some more altitude and upgrade my attitude?

17.00

18.00

19.00

What beliefs are holding me back and how can I upgrade those?

20.00

date:

| Old Habit > | New Habit > | New Actions > | New Affirmation / Mantra |

My goals for the next week

Weekly Planner

My mantra for this week is ....

4 Major Goals I'm Focused On This Week

| 1. | 2. | 3. | 4. |

| Projects & appointments for this week | Target date | Actions for this week | Target date |

monday

tuesday

wednesday

thursday

friday

saturday

sunday

fun space

....
....
....

Today I AM open to the possibility of...

What I love about my work is...

Today I AM inspired to take these actions...

1.
2.
3.

I have a winning mindset and...

I AM
I AM
I AM
I AM

What have I learned today?

How was my mindset today?

What new habit do I want to adopt into my life?

How did I give value today?

date:

reminders

....
....
....
....
....
....
....

☐ **M & V** meditation & visualisation ☐ **I** inspiration
☐ **E** exercise ☐ ....

6.00
7.00
8.00
9.00
10.00
11.00
12.00
13.00
14.00
15.00
16.00
17.00
18.00
19.00
20.00

genius space

....
....
....

I AM present

Today, it would be fun to...

I AM so grateful for the simple things like...

What is the best course of action to take today?

1.
2.
3.

Today I AM creative and...

I AM
I AM
I AM
I AM

What was fantastic about today?

What skill can I develop further?

What new mindset do I want to adopt into my life?

What did I do really well today?

M & V meditation & visualisation
I inspiration
E exercise
....

6.00
7.00
8.00
9.00
10.00
11.00
12.00
13.00
14.00
15.00
16.00
17.00
18.00
19.00
20.00

date:

dream space

....
....
....

Today I would love....

Today I AM so grateful for...

My top 3 inspired actions for today are...

1.
2.
3.

My intentions for today are...

I AM
I AM
I AM
I AM

What was great about today?

What did I learn today?

After today, what behaviour do I want to upgrade?

What strengths did I use today?

date:

reminders

....
....
....
....
....
....
....

☐ **M & V** meditation & visualisation ☐ **I** inspiration
☐ **E** exercise ☐ ....

6.00
7.00
8.00
9.00
10.00
11.00
12.00
13.00
14.00
15.00
16.00
17.00
18.00
19.00
20.00

creative space

....
....
....

What if (insert possibility)....

Appreciation & Gratitude list...

M & V meditation & visualisation
I inspiration
E exercise

Today, I AM most inspired to do these actions...

1.
2.
3.

The mindset I wish to create today is...

I AM
I AM
I AM
I AM

What did I enjoy about today?

What challenged me today that I can grow from?

What would I like to create instead?

What did I do really well today?

6.00
7.00
8.00
9.00
10.00
11.00
12.00
13.00
14.00
15.00
16.00
17.00
18.00
19.00
20.00

date:

ideas space

....
....
....

Today I accept that....

The things I AM grateful for in my life are...

Today, I would love to do these actions...

1.
2.
3.

Today I AM focusing on being...

I AM
I AM
I AM
I AM

What went well today?

What could I have handled differently today?

How can I open up to new ways of doing things?

What am I proud of about today?

date:

reminders

....
....
....
....
....
....
....

☐ **M & V** meditation & visualisation   ☐ **I** inspiration
☐ **E** exercise   ☐ ....

6.00
7.00
8.00
9.00
10.00
11.00
12.00
13.00
14.00
15.00
16.00
17.00
18.00
19.00
20.00

thoughts space

....
....
....

Today I AM going to create...

Gratitude is Wisdom...

☐ **M & V** meditation & visualisation
☐ **I** inspiration
☐ **E** exercise
....

Today, I feel inspired to do...

1.
2.
3.

I create my day with my thoughts, therefore...

I AM
I AM
I AM
I AM

What did I love about today?

In what area would I like to grow?

What would I like to let go of?

How did I show leadership today?

	6.00
	7.00
	8.00
	9.00
	10.00
	11.00
	12.00
	13.00
	14.00
	15.00
	16.00
	17.00
	18.00
	19.00
	20.00

date:

My week in review

Weekly Check-in

What projects have I completed this week?

☐ Review Greatness Blueprint

☐ Review Purpose Statement

What's going well and why is it?

☐ Update 90 Day Planner

☐ Add Actions To Weekly Planner

☐ Plan Your Week

What's most challenging and how can I turn it into an opportunity?

8.00

9.00

What is one thing I can do next week that will create the biggest results in my life?

10.00

11.00

What am I happy about right now?

12.00

13.00

14.00

How am I using my time? How can I prioritise better?

15.00

16.00

GET SOME ALTITUDE Where is my current attitude on a scale from 1-10? How can I get some more altitude and upgrade my attitude?

17.00

18.00

19.00

What fears are holding me back and how can I overcome those?

20.00

date:

| Old Habit > | New Habit > | New Actions > | New Affirmation / Mantra |

My goals for the next week

Weekly Planner

My mantra for this week is ....

4 Major Goals I'm Focused On This Week

| 1. | 2. | 3. | 4. |

| Projects & appointments for this week | Target date | Actions for this week | Target date |

monday

tuesday

wednesday

thursday

friday

saturday

sunday

open space

....
....
....

Today I AM going to enjoy...

When I AM grateful I open up to more...

What would I do today, if it was my last?

1.
2.
3.

Today...
I AM
I AM
I AM
I AM

What was interesting about today?

What habit would I like to develop after today?

What beliefs would I like to upgrade?

What strengths did I use today?

date:

reminders

....
....
....
....
....
....
....

☐ **M & V** meditation & visualisation   ☐ **I** inspiration
☐ **E** exercise   ☐ ....

6.00
7.00
8.00
9.00
10.00
11.00
12.00
13.00
14.00
15.00
16.00
17.00
18.00
19.00
20.00

invention space

....
....
....

Today is my opportunity to...

Today, I give thanks for...

M & V meditation & visualisation
I inspiration
E exercise
....

My inspired actions for today are...

1.
2.
3.

6.00
7.00
8.00
9.00
10.00
11.00

Today I honor how I feel and...

I AM
I AM
I AM
I AM

12.00
13.00

What was fun about today?

14.00
15.00

What was today's lesson?

16.00
17.00

What new behaviour can I adopt into my life?

18.00
19.00

What did I succeed at...

20.00

date:

fun space

....
....
....

Today I AM open to the possibility of...

What I love about my work is...

Today I AM inspired to take these actions...
1.
2.
3.

I have a winning mindset and...
I AM
I AM
I AM
I AM

What have I learned today?

How was my mindset today?

What new habit do I want to adopt into my life?

How did I give value today?

date:

reminders

....
....
....
....
....
....
....

☐ **M & V** meditation & visualisation   ☐ **I** inspiration
☐ **E** exercise   ☐ ....

6.00
7.00
8.00
9.00
10.00
11.00
12.00
13.00
14.00
15.00
16.00
17.00
18.00
19.00
20.00

… genius space

……………………………………………………………………
……………………………………………………………………
……………………………………………………………………

Today, it would be fun to…

I AM so grateful for the simple things like…

M & V meditation & visualisation
I inspiration
E exercise
………………

What is the best course of action to take today?

1.
2.
3.

Today I AM creative and…

I AM
I AM
I AM
I AM

What was fantastic about today?

What skill can I develop further?

What new mindset do I want to adopt into my life?

What did I do really well today?

6.00
7.00
8.00
9.00
10.00
11.00
12.00
13.00
14.00
15.00
16.00
17.00
18.00
19.00
20.00

date:

dream space

....
....
....

Today I would love....

Today I AM so grateful for...

My top 3 inspired actions for today are...

1.
2.
3.

My intentions for today are...

I AM
I AM
I AM
I AM

What was great about today?

What did I learn today?

After today, what behaviour do I want to upgrade?

What strengths did I use today?

date:

reminders

....
....
....
....
....
....
....

☐ **M & V** meditation & visualisation ☐ **I** inspiration
☐ **E** exercise ☐ ....

6.00
....
7.00
....
8.00
....
9.00
....
10.00
....
11.00
....
12.00
....
13.00
....
14.00
....
15.00
....
16.00
....
17.00
....
18.00
....
19.00
....
20.00
....

creative space

....
....
....

What if (insert possibility)....

Appreciation & Gratitude list...

☐ **M & V** meditation & visualisation ☐ **I** inspiration
☐ **E** exercise ....

Today, I AM most inspired to do these actions...

1.
2.
3.

The mindset I wish to create today is...

I AM
I AM
I AM
I AM

What did I enjoy about today?

What challenged me today that I can grow from?

What would I like to create instead?

What did I do really well today?

.... 6.00
.... 7.00
.... 8.00
.... 9.00
.... 10.00
.... 11.00
.... 12.00
.... 13.00
.... 14.00
.... 15.00
.... 16.00
.... 17.00
.... 18.00
.... 19.00
.... 20.00

date:

My week in review

Weekly Check-in

What have I achieved on my greatness blueprint this week?

☐ Review Greatness Blueprint

☐ Review Purpose Statement

Where am I seeing the desired results & why?

☐ Update 90 Day Planner

☐ Add Actions To Weekly Planner

What do I need to start or stop?

☐ Plan Your Week

8.00

9.00

What is one thing I can do next week that will create the biggest results in my life?

10.00

11.00

12.00

Where can I be a better leader?

13.00

14.00

Do I need to upgrade my communication skills? How can I be better?

15.00

16.00

GET SOME ALTITUDE Where is my current attitude on a scale from 1 -10? How can I get some more altitude and upgrade my attitude?

17.00

18.00

19.00

What negative attitudes are holding me back and how can I overcome those?

20.00

date:

| Old Habit > | New Habit > | New Actions > | New Affirmation / Mantra |

My goals for the next week

My mantra for this week is
....

Weekly Planner

4 Major Goals I'm Focused On This Week

| 1. | 2. | 3. | 4. |

Projects & appointments for this week	Target date	Actions for this week	Target date
monday			
tuesday			
wednesday			
thursday			
friday			
saturday			
sunday			

ideas space

....

....

....

Today I accept that....

The things I AM grateful for in my life are...

Today, I would love to do these actions...

1.
2.
3.

Today I AM focusing on being...

I AM

I AM

I AM

I AM

What went well today?

What could I have handled differently today?

How can I open up to new ways of doing things?

What am I proud of about today?

date:

reminders

....

....

....

....

....

....

....

....

☐ **M & V** meditation & visualisation ☐ **I** inspiration
☐ **E** exercise ☐ ....

6.00
7.00
8.00
9.00
10.00
11.00
12.00
13.00
14.00
15.00
16.00
17.00
18.00
19.00
20.00

thoughts space

....
....
....

Today I AM going to create...

....
....
....
....
....
....
....
....

Gratitude is Wisdom...

☐ **M & V** meditation & visualisation
☐ **I** inspiration
☐ **E** exercise
☐ ....

Today, I feel inspired to do...

1.
2.
3.

	6.00
	7.00
	8.00
	9.00
	10.00
	11.00
	12.00
	13.00
	14.00
	15.00
	16.00
	17.00
	18.00
	19.00
	20.00

I create my day with my thoughts, therefore...

I AM
I AM
I AM
I AM

What did I love about today?

In what area would I like to grow?

What would I like to let go of?

How did I show leadership today?

date:

open space

....
....
....

Today I AM going to enjoy...

When I AM grateful I open up to more...

What would I do today, if it was my last?

1.
2.
3.

Today...
I AM
I AM
I AM
I AM

What was interesting about today?

What habit would I like to develop after today?

What beliefs would I like to upgrade?

What strengths did I use today?

date:

reminders

....
....
....
....
....
....

☐ **M & V** meditation & visualisation   ☐ **I** inspiration
☐ **E** exercise   ☐ ....

6.00
7.00
8.00
9.00
10.00
11.00
12.00
13.00
14.00
15.00
16.00
17.00
18.00
19.00
20.00

invention space

....
....
....

Today is my opportunity to...

Today, I give thanks for...

M & V meditation & visualisation
I inspiration
E exercise

My inspired actions for today are...

1.
2.
3.

Today I honor how I feel and...

I AM
I AM
I AM
I AM

What was fun about today?

What was today's lesson?

What new behaviour can I adopt into my life?

What did I succeed at...

6.00
7.00
8.00
9.00
10.00
11.00
12.00
13.00
14.00
15.00
16.00
17.00
18.00
19.00
20.00

date:

fun space

....
....
....

Today I AM open to the possibility of...

What I love about my work is...

Today I AM inspired to take these actions...

1.
2.
3.

I have a winning mindset and...

I AM
I AM
I AM
I AM

What have I learned today?

How was my mindset today?

What new habit do I want to adopt into my life?

How did I give value today?

date:

reminders

....
....
....
....
....
....
....

☐ **M & V** meditation & visualisation   ☐ **I** inspiration
☐ **E** exercise

6.00
7.00
8.00
9.00
10.00
11.00
12.00
13.00
14.00
15.00
16.00
17.00
18.00
19.00
20.00

genius space

....
....
....

Today, it would be fun to...

I AM so grateful for the simple things like...

M & V meditation & visualisation
I inspiration
E exercise
....

What is the best course of action to take today?

1.
2.
3.

Today I AM creative and...

I AM
I AM
I AM
I AM

6.00
7.00
8.00
9.00
10.00
11.00
12.00

What was fantastic about today?

13.00
14.00

What skill can I develop further?

15.00
16.00

What new mindset do I want to adopt into my life?

17.00
18.00

What did I do really well today?

19.00
20.00

date:

My week in review

Weekly Check-in

What major goals have I achieved this month?

☐ Review Greatness Blueprint

☐ Review Purpose Statement

Where am I having success and why?

☐ Update 90 Day Planner

☐ Add Actions To Weekly Planner

☐ Plan Your Week

What are the biggest distractions in my life and how can I remove them?

8.00

9.00

What is one thing I can do next week that will create the biggest results in my life?

10.00

11.00

What am I committed to achieving in my life right now?

12.00

13.00

14.00

date:

What is my home and work environment like? Does it inspire me?

15.00

16.00

GET SOME ALTITUDE Where is my current attitude on a scale from 1 -10? How can I get some more altitude and upgrade my attitude?

17.00

18.00

19.00

What disempowering thoughts are holding me back and how can I upgrade those?

20.00

Old Habit >	New Habit >	New Actions >	New Affirmation / Mantra

My goals for the next week

Weekly Planner

My mantra for this week is ....

4 Major Goals I'm Focused On This Week

| 1. | 2. | 3. | 4. |

Projects & appointments for this week	Target date	Actions for this week	Target date

monday

tuesday

wednesday

thursday

friday

saturday

sunday

ideas space

....
....
....

Today I accept that....

The things I AM grateful for in my life are...

Today, I would love to do these actions...

1.
2.
3.

Today I AM focusing on being...

I AM
I AM
I AM
I AM

What went well today?

What could I have handled differently today?

How can I open up to new ways of doing things?

What am I proud of about today?

date:

reminders

....
....
....
....
....
....
....

☐ **M & V** meditation & visualisation   ☐ **I** inspiration
☐ **E** exercise   ☐ ....

6.00
7.00
8.00
9.00
10.00
11.00
12.00
13.00
14.00
15.00
16.00
17.00
18.00
19.00
20.00

thoughts space

....
....
....

Today I AM going to create...

Gratitude is Wisdom...

M & V meditation & visualisation
I inspiration
E exercise ....

Today, I feel inspired to do...

1.
2.
3.

I create my day with my thoughts, therefore...

I AM
I AM
I AM
I AM

What did I love about today?

In what area would I like to grow?

What would I like to let go of?

How did I show leadership today?

6.00
7.00
8.00
9.00
10.00
11.00
12.00
13.00
14.00
15.00
16.00
17.00
18.00
19.00
20.00

date:

open space

....
....
....

Today I AM going to enjoy...

When I AM grateful I open up to more...

What would I do today, if it was my last?

1.
2.
3.

Today...

I AM
I AM
I AM
I AM

What was interesting about today?

What habit would I like to develop after today?

What beliefs would I like to upgrade?

What strengths did I use today?

date:

reminders

....
....
....
....
....
....
....

☐ **M & V** meditation & visualisation ☐ **I** inspiration
☐ **E** exercise ☐ ....

6.00
7.00
8.00
9.00
10.00
11.00
12.00
13.00
14.00
15.00
16.00
17.00
18.00
19.00
20.00

invention space

I AM creative

M & V meditation & visualisation
E exercise
I inspiration

6.00	
7.00	
8.00	
9.00	
10.00	
11.00	
12.00	
13.00	
14.00	
15.00	
16.00	
17.00	
18.00	
19.00	
20.00	

Today is my opportunity to...

Today, I give thanks for...

My inspired actions for today are...

1.
2.
3.

Today I honor how I feel and...

I AM
I AM
I AM
I AM

What was fun about today?

What was today's lesson?

What new behaviour can I adopt into my life?

What did I succeed at...

date:

fun space

....
....
....

Today I AM open to the possibility of...

What I love about my work is...

Today I AM inspired to take these actions...

1.
2.
3.

I have a winning mindset and...

I AM
I AM
I AM
I AM

What have I learned today?

How was my mindset today?

What new habit do I want to adopt into my life?

How did I give value today?

date:

reminders

....
....
....
....
....
....
....

☐ **M & V** meditation & visualisation   ☐ **I** inspiration
☐ **E** exercise   ☐ ....

6.00
....
7.00
....
8.00
....
9.00
....
10.00
....
11.00
....
12.00
....
13.00
....
14.00
....
15.00
....
16.00
....
17.00
....
18.00
....
19.00
....
20.00
....

genius space

....
....
....

Today, it would be fun to...

I AM so grateful for the simple things like...

What is the best course of action to take today?

1.
2.
3.

Today I AM creative and...

I AM
I AM
I AM
I AM

What was fantastic about today?

What skill can I develop further?

What new mindset do I want to adopt into my life?

What did I do really well today?

M & V meditation & visualisation
I inspiration
E exercise

- 6.00
- 7.00
- 8.00
- 9.00
- 10.00
- 11.00
- 12.00
- 13.00
- 14.00
- 15.00
- 16.00
- 17.00
- 18.00
- 19.00
- 20.00

date:

90 Day Check-in

Welcome to your 90-day check-in! It's time to celebrate your achievements, identify what needs attention, check your life balance, and set your focus for the next 90 days. Use the answers to the questions to plan your next quarter and adjust your goals, intentions, and actions accordingly. Transfer these to Your Achievements page to keep inspired and motivated about your progress.

What major goals have I completed this past 90 days?
What am I happy about?

....
....

How can I align more with my Greatness Blueprint and overall purpose? Does my vision still inspire me or do I need to upgrade my strategy?

....
....

What would I love to create in the next 90 days?
What goal or project am I focusing on?

....
....

What new mindset do I wish to develop?
What is no longer acceptable to me?

....
....

How do I feel about the 8 areas of my life?
How can I become more balanced and happy?
What areas of my life need attention?

....
....

Am I embracing change or resisting it?
How can I open up to more expansion?

....
....

Do I have a good team of people around me?
How can I surround myself with great people?
Who is my mentor?

....
....

What else have I noticed about my life in the last 90 days?

....
....

☐ Review Greatness Blueprint   ☐ Review Your Yearly Planner   ☐ Plan Your Week

☐ Review Purpose Statement   ☐ Complete Next 90 Day Planner   ☐ Celebrate Your Progress!

My goals for the next 90 days

90 Day Planner

Goal:

Project:

Target date:

Actions to complete this goal:

1.
2.
3.
4.

Why I'd love to achieve this goal:

How will I feel when I've reached this goal?

Goal:

Project:

Target date:

Actions to complete this goal:

1.
2.
3.
4.

Why I'd love to achieve this goal:

How will I feel when I've reached this goal?

Goal:

Project:

Target date:

Actions to complete this goal:

1.
2.
3.
4.

Why I'd love to achieve this goal:

How will I feel when I've reached this goal?

Goal:

Project:

Target date:

Actions to complete this goal:

1.
2.
3.
4.

Why I'd love to achieve this goal:

How will I feel when I've reached this goal?

Your past is not your potential. In any hour you can choose to liberate the future.

Marilyn Ferguson

Our aspirations are our possibilities.

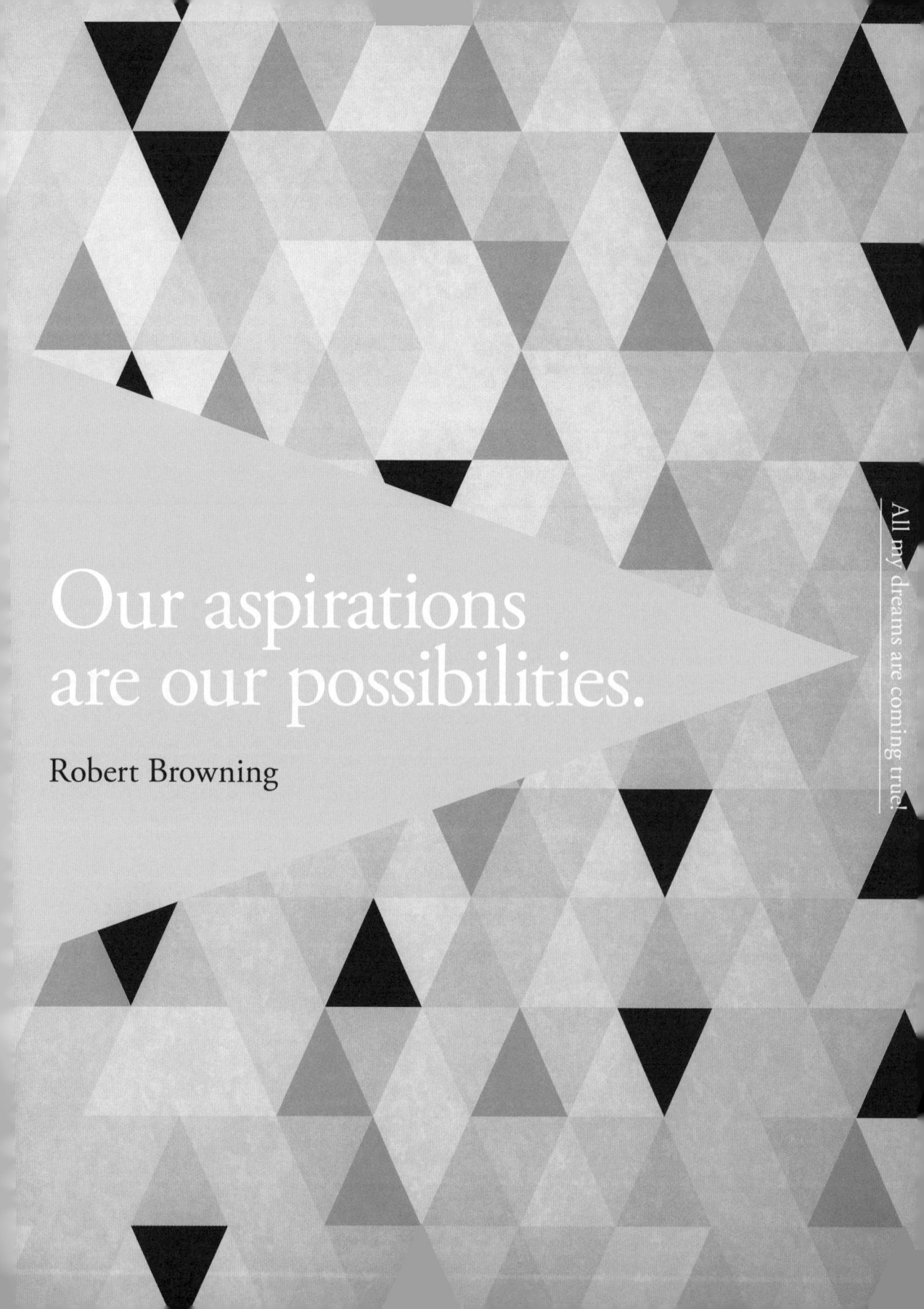

Robert Browning

All my dreams are coming true!

My Genius Space

My goals for the next week

Weekly Planner

My mantra for this week is ....

4 Major Goals I'm Focused On This Week

| 1. | 2. | 3. | 4. |

Projects & appointments for this week	Target date	Actions for this week	Target date

monday

tuesday

wednesday

thursday

friday

saturday

sunday

dream space

....
....
....

Today I would love....

Today I AM so grateful for...

My top 3 inspired actions for today are...

1.
2.
3.

My intentions for today are...

I AM
I AM
I AM
I AM

What was great about today?

What did I learn today?

After today, what behaviour do I want to upgrade?

What strengths did I use today?

date:

reminders

....
....
....
....
....
....
....

I AM in love with life

☐ **M & V** meditation & visualisation ☐ **I** inspiration
☐ **E** exercise ☐ ....

6.00
7.00
8.00
9.00
10.00
11.00
12.00
13.00
14.00
15.00
16.00
17.00
18.00
19.00
20.00

creative space

....
....
....

What if (insert possibility)....

Appreciation & Gratitude list...

Today, I AM most inspired to do these actions...

1.
2.
3.

The mindset I wish to create today is...

I AM
I AM
I AM
I AM

What did I enjoy about today?

What challenged me today that I can grow from?

What would I like to create instead?

What did I do really well today?

M & V
meditation & visualisation

I
inspiration

E
exercise

....

- 6.00
- 7.00
- 8.00
- 9.00
- 10.00
- 11.00
- 12.00
- 13.00
- 14.00
- 15.00
- 16.00
- 17.00
- 18.00
- 19.00
- 20.00

date:

ideas space

....

....

....

Today I accept that....

The things I AM grateful for in my life are...

Today, I would love to do these actions...

1.
2.
3.

Today I AM focusing on being...

I AM

I AM

I AM

I AM

What went well today?

What could I have handled differently today?

How can I open up to new ways of doing things?

What am I proud of about today?

date:

reminders

....

....

....

....

....

....

....

☐ **M & V** meditation & visualisation ☐ **I** inspiration

☐ **E** exercise ☐ ....

6.00
7.00
8.00
9.00
10.00
11.00
12.00
13.00
14.00
15.00
16.00
17.00
18.00
19.00
20.00

thoughts space

....
....
....

Today I AM going to create...

Gratitude is Wisdom...

M & V
meditation & visualisation

I
inspiration

E
exercise

Today, I feel inspired to do...

1.
2.
3.

6.00
7.00
8.00
9.00
10.00
11.00
12.00
13.00
14.00
15.00
16.00
17.00
18.00
19.00
20.00

I create my day with my thoughts, therefore...

I AM
I AM
I AM
I AM

What did I love about today?

In what area would I like to grow?

What would I like to let go of?

How did I show leadership today?

date:

open space

....
....
....

Today I AM going to enjoy...

When I AM grateful I open up to more...

What would I do today, if it was my last?

1.
2.
3.

Today...

I AM
I AM
I AM
I AM

What was interesting about today?

What habit would I like to develop after today?

What beliefs would I like to upgrade?

What strengths did I use today?

date:

reminders

....
....
....
....
....
....
....

☐ **M & V** meditation & visualisation   ☐ **I** inspiration
☐ **E** exercise   ☐ ....

6.00
7.00
8.00
9.00
10.00
11.00
12.00
13.00
14.00
15.00
16.00
17.00
18.00
19.00
20.00

invention space

....
....
....

Today is my opportunity to...

....
....
....
....
....
....

Today, I give thanks for...

☐ **M & V**
  meditation & visualisation
☐ **I**
  inspiration
☐ **E**
  exercise
  ....

My inspired actions for today are...

1.
2.
3.

6.00	
7.00	
8.00	
9.00	
10.00	
11.00	
12.00	
13.00	
14.00	
15.00	
16.00	
17.00	
18.00	
19.00	
20.00	

Today I honor how I feel and...

I AM
I AM
I AM
I AM

What was fun about today?

What was today's lesson?

What new behaviour can I adopt into my life?

What did I succeed at...

date:

My week in review

Weekly Check-in

What have I achieved this week?

☐ Review Greatness Blueprint

☐ Review Purpose Statement

What's working and why is it working?

☐ Update 90 Day Planner

☐ Add Actions To Weekly Planner

☐ Plan Your Week

What's not working and what am I willing to do about it?

8.00

9.00

What is one thing I can do next week that will create the biggest results in my life?

10.00

11.00

What do I need to make a decision about?

12.00

13.00

14.00

Have I had fun this week? How can I have more fun?

15.00

16.00

GET SOME ALTITUDE Where is my current attitude on a scale from 1-10? How can I get some more altitude and upgrade my attitude?

17.00

18.00

19.00

What beliefs are holding me back and how can I upgrade those?

20.00

date:

Old Habit >	New Habit >	New Actions >	New Affirmation / Mantra

My goals for the next week

Weekly Planner

My mantra for this week is ....

4 Major Goals I'm Focused On This Week

| 1. | 2. | 3. | 4. |

| Projects & appointments for this week | Target date | Actions for this week | Target date |

- monday
- tuesday
- wednesday
- thursday
- friday
- saturday
- sunday

fun space

....
....
....

Today I AM open to the possibility of...

What I love about my work is...

Today I AM inspired to take these actions...

1.
2.
3.

I have a winning mindset and...

I AM
I AM
I AM
I AM

What have I learned today?

How was my mindset today?

What new habit do I want to adopt into my life?

How did I give value today?

date:

reminders

....
....
....
....
....
....
....

☐ **M & V** meditation & visualisation   ☐ **I** inspiration
☐ **E** exercise   ☐ ....

6.00
7.00
8.00
9.00
10.00
11.00
12.00
13.00
14.00
15.00
16.00
17.00
18.00
19.00
20.00

genius space

....
....
....

Today, it would be fun to...

I AM so grateful for the simple things like...

☐ M & V
meditation & visualisation

☐ I
inspiration

☐ E
exercise

What is the best course of action to take today?

1.
2.
3.

6.00
7.00
8.00
9.00
10.00
11.00
12.00
13.00
14.00
15.00
16.00
17.00
18.00
19.00
20.00

Today I AM creative and...

I AM
I AM
I AM
I AM

What was fantastic about today?

What skill can I develop further?

What new mindset do I want to adopt into my life?

What did I do really well today?

date:

dream space

....
....
....

Today I would love....

Today I AM so grateful for...

My top 3 inspired actions for today are...

1.
2.
3.

My intentions for today are...

I AM
I AM
I AM
I AM

What was great about today?

What did I learn today?

After today, what behaviour do I want to upgrade?

What strengths did I use today?

date:

reminders

....
....
....
....
....
....
....

☐ **M & V** meditation & visualisation   ☐ **I** inspiration
☐ **E** exercise   ☐ ....

6.00
7.00
8.00
9.00
10.00
11.00
12.00
13.00
14.00
15.00
16.00
17.00
18.00
19.00
20.00

creative space

....
....
....

What if (insert possibility)....

Appreciation & Gratitude list...

☐ M & V
  meditation & visualisation
☐ I
  inspiration
☐ E
  exercise
....

Today, I AM most inspired to do these actions...

1.
2.
3.

The mindset I wish to create today is...

I AM
I AM
I AM
I AM

What did I enjoy about today?

6.00
7.00
8.00
9.00
10.00
11.00
12.00
13.00
14.00

What challenged me today that I can grow from?

15.00
16.00

What would I like to create instead?

17.00
18.00

What did I do really well today?

19.00
20.00

date:

ideas space

....

....

....

Today I accept that....

The things I AM grateful for in my life are...

Today, I would love to do these actions...

1.
2.
3.

Today I AM focusing on being...

I AM

I AM

I AM

I AM

What went well today?

What could I have handled differently today?

How can I open up to new ways of doing things?

What am I proud of about today?

date:

reminders

....

....

....

....

....

....

....

☐ **M & V** meditation & visualisation ☐ **I** inspiration
☐ **E** exercise ☐ ....

6.00
7.00
8.00
9.00
10.00
11.00
12.00
13.00
14.00
15.00
16.00
17.00
18.00
19.00
20.00

thoughts space

....
....
....

Today I AM going to create...

Gratitude is Wisdom...

Today, I feel inspired to do...

1.
2.
3.

I create my day with my thoughts, therefore...

I AM
I AM
I AM
I AM

What did I love about today?

In what area would I like to grow?

What would I like to let go of?

How did I show leadership today?

....
....
....
....
....
....
....
....
....

M & V meditation & visualisation
I inspiration
E exercise

....

	6.00
	7.00
	8.00
	9.00
	10.00
	11.00
	12.00
	13.00
	14.00
	15.00
	16.00
	17.00
	18.00
	19.00
	20.00

date:

My week in review

Weekly Check-in

What projects have I completed this week?

☐ Review Greatness Blueprint

☐ Review Purpose Statement

☐ Update 90 Day Planner

What's going well and why is it?

☐ Add Actions To Weekly Planner

☐ Plan Your Week

What's most challenging and how can I turn it into an opportunity?

What is one thing I can do next week that will create the biggest results in my life?

What am I happy about right now?

How am I using my time? How can I prioritise better?

GET SOME ALTITUDE Where is my current attitude on a scale from 1-10? How can I get some more altitude and upgrade my attitude?

What fears are holding me back and how can I overcome those?

8.00
9.00
10.00
11.00
12.00
13.00
14.00
15.00
16.00
17.00
18.00
19.00
20.00

date:

Old Habit > | New Habit > | New Actions > | New Affirmation / Mantra

My goals for the next week

Weekly Planner

My mantra for this week is ....

4 Major Goals I'm Focused On This Week

1.
2.
3.
4.

Projects & appointments for this week	Target date	Actions for this week	Target date

monday

tuesday

wednesday

thursday

friday

saturday

sunday

open space

....

....

....

Today I AM going to enjoy...

When I AM grateful I open up to more...

What would I do today, if it was my last?
1.
2.
3.

Today...
I AM
I AM
I AM
I AM

What was interesting about today?

What habit would I like to develop after today?

What beliefs would I like to upgrade?

What strengths did I use today?

date:

reminders

....
....
....
....
....
....
....

☐ **M & V** meditation & visualisation   ☐ **I** inspiration
☐ **E** exercise   ☐ ....

6.00
7.00
8.00
9.00
10.00
11.00
12.00
13.00
14.00
15.00
16.00
17.00
18.00
19.00
20.00

invention space

....
....
....

Today is my opportunity to...

Today, I give thanks for...

My inspired actions for today are...

1.
2.
3.

Today I honor how I feel and...

I AM
I AM
I AM
I AM

What was fun about today?

What was today's lesson?

What new behaviour can I adopt into my life?

What did I succeed at...

M & V
meditation & visualisation

I
inspiration

E
exercise

....

6.00
7.00
8.00
9.00
10.00
11.00
12.00
13.00
14.00
15.00
16.00
17.00
18.00
19.00
20.00

date:

fun space

....

....

....

Today I AM open to the possibility of...

What I love about my work is...

Today I AM inspired to take these actions...
1.
2.
3.

I have a winning mindset and...

I AM

I AM

I AM

I AM

What have I learned today?

How was my mindset today?

What new habit do I want to adopt into my life?

How did I give value today?

date:

reminders

....

....

....

....

....

....

....

☐ **M & V** meditation & visualisation   ☐ **I** inspiration

☐ **E** exercise   ☐ ....

6.00
....
7.00
....
8.00
....
9.00
....
10.00
....
11.00
....
12.00
....
13.00
....
14.00
....
15.00
....
16.00
....
17.00
....
18.00
....
19.00
....
20.00
....

genius space

....
....
....

Today, it would be fun to...

I AM so grateful for the simple things like...

....
....
....
....
....
....
....

☐ M & V
  meditation & visualisation
☐ I
  inspiration
☐ E
  exercise
☐ ....

What is the best course of action to take today?

1.
2.
3.

Today I AM creative and...

I AM
I AM
I AM
I AM

6.00
7.00
8.00
9.00
10.00
11.00

What was fantastic about today?

12.00
13.00
14.00

What skill can I develop further?

15.00
16.00

What new mindset do I want to adopt into my life?

17.00
18.00

What did I do really well today?

19.00
20.00

date:

dream space

....
....
....

Today I would love....

Today I AM so grateful for...

My top 3 inspired actions for today are...

1.
2.
3.

My intentions for today are...

I AM
I AM
I AM
I AM

What was great about today?

What did I learn today?

After today, what behaviour do I want to upgrade?

What strengths did I use today?

date:

reminders

....
....
....
....
....
....
....

☐ **M & V** meditation & visualisation   ☐ **I** inspiration
☐ **E** exercise   ☐ ....

6.00
7.00
8.00
9.00
10.00
11.00
12.00
13.00
14.00
15.00
16.00
17.00
18.00
19.00
20.00

I AM
peaceful

creative space

....
....
....
.... What if (insert possibility)....
....
....
.... Appreciation & Gratitude list...
....

M & V		I	
meditation & visualisation		inspiration	
E			....
exercise			

Today, I AM most inspired to do these actions...

1.
2.
3.

The mindset I wish to create today is...

I AM
I AM
I AM
I AM

What did I enjoy about today?

What challenged me today that I can grow from?

What would I like to create instead?

What did I do really well today?

6.00
7.00
8.00
9.00
10.00
11.00
12.00
13.00
14.00
15.00
16.00
17.00
18.00
19.00
20.00

date:

My week in review

Weekly Check-in

What have I achieved on my greatness blueprint this week?

☐ Review Greatness Blueprint

☐ Review Purpose Statement

Where am I seeing the desired results & why?

☐ Update 90 Day Planner

☐ Add Actions To Weekly Planner

☐ Plan Your Week

What do I need to start or stop?

8.00

9.00

What is one thing I can do next week that will create the biggest results in my life?

10.00

11.00

12.00

Where can I be a better leader?

13.00

14.00

Do I need to upgrade my communication skills? How can I be better?

15.00

16.00

17.00

GET SOME ALTITUDE Where is my current attitude on a scale from 1-10? How can I get some more altitude and upgrade my attitude?

18.00

19.00

What negative attitudes are holding me back and how can I overcome those?

20.00

date:

| Old Habit > | New Habit > | New Actions > | New Affirmation / Mantra |

My goals for the next week

My mantra for this week is ....

Weekly Planner

4 Major Goals I'm Focused On This Week

| 1. | 2. | 3. | 4. |

| Projects & appointments for this week | Target date | Actions for this week | Target date |

monday

tuesday

wednesday

thursday

friday

saturday

sunday

ideas space

....
....
....

Today I accept that....

The things I AM grateful for in my life are...

Today, I would love to do these actions...

1.
2.
3.

Today I AM focusing on being...

I AM
I AM
I AM
I AM

What went well today?

What could I have handled differently today?

How can I open up to new ways of doing things?

What am I proud of about today?

date:

reminders

....
....
....
....
....
....
....

☐ **M & V** meditation & visualisation   ☐ **I** inspiration
☐ **E** exercise   ☐ ....

6.00
7.00
8.00
9.00
10.00
11.00
12.00
13.00
14.00
15.00
16.00
17.00
18.00
19.00
20.00

thoughts space

....
....
....

Today I AM going to create...

Gratitude is Wisdom...

Today, I feel inspired to do...

1.
2.
3.

I create my day with my thoughts, therefore...

I AM
I AM
I AM
I AM

What did I love about today?

In what area would I like to grow?

What would I like to let go of?

How did I show leadership today?

....
....
....
....
....
....
....
....
....

☐ **M & V** meditation & visualisation
☐ **I** inspiration
☐ **E** exercise ....

- 6.00
- 7.00
- 8.00
- 9.00
- 10.00
- 11.00
- 12.00
- 13.00
- 14.00
- 15.00
- 16.00
- 17.00
- 18.00
- 19.00
- 20.00

date:

open space

....
....
....

Today I AM going to enjoy...

When I AM grateful I open up to more...

What would I do today, if it was my last?

1.
2.
3.

Today...
I AM
I AM
I AM
I AM

What was interesting about today?

What habit would I like to develop after today?

What beliefs would I like to upgrade?

What strengths did I use today?

date:

reminders

....
....
....
....
....
....
....

☐ **M & V** meditation & visualisation ☐ **I** inspiration
☐ **E** exercise ☐ ....

6.00
7.00
8.00
9.00
10.00
11.00
12.00
13.00
14.00
15.00
16.00
17.00
18.00
19.00
20.00

invention space

....
....
....

Today is my opportunity to...

Today, I give thanks for...

M & V meditation & visualisation
I inspiration
E exercise
....

My inspired actions for today are...

1.
2.
3.

Today I honor how I feel and...

I AM
I AM
I AM
I AM

What was fun about today?

What was today's lesson?

What new behaviour can I adopt into my life?

What did I succeed at...

date:

6.00
7.00
8.00
9.00
10.00
11.00
12.00
13.00
14.00
15.00
16.00
17.00
18.00
19.00
20.00

fun space

....
....
....

Today I AM open to the possibility of...

What I love about my work is...

Today I AM inspired to take these actions...

1.
2.
3.

I have a winning mindset and...

I AM
I AM
I AM
I AM

What have I learned today?

How was my mindset today?

What new habit do I want to adopt into my life?

How did I give value today?

date:

reminders

....
....
....
....
....
....
....
....

☐ **M & V** meditation & visualisation   ☐ **I** inspiration
☐ **E** exercise   ☐ ....

6.00
7.00
8.00
9.00
10.00
11.00
12.00
13.00
14.00
15.00
16.00
17.00
18.00
19.00
20.00

genius space

....
....
....

Today, it would be fun to...

I AM so grateful for the simple things like...

What is the best course of action to take today?

1.
2.
3.

Today I AM creative and...

I AM
I AM
I AM
I AM

What was fantastic about today?

What skill can I develop further?

What new mindset do I want to adopt into my life?

What did I do really well today?

M & V meditation & visualisation
I inspiration
E exercise

6.00
7.00
8.00
9.00
10.00
11.00
12.00
13.00
14.00
15.00
16.00
17.00
18.00
19.00
20.00

date:

My week in review

Weekly Check-in

What major goals have I achieved this month?

☐ Review Greatness Blueprint

☐ Review Purpose Statement

Where am I having success and why?

☐ Update 90 Day Planner

☐ Add Actions To Weekly Planner

☐ Plan Your Week

What are the biggest distractions in my life and how can I remove them?

8.00

9.00

What is one thing I can do next week that will create the biggest results in my life?

10.00

11.00

What am I committed to achieving in my life right now?

12.00

13.00

14.00

What is my home and work environment like? Does it inspire me?

15.00

16.00

GET SOME ALTITUDE Where is my current attitude on a scale from 1-10? How can I get some more altitude and upgrade my attitude?

17.00

18.00

19.00

What disempowering thoughts are holding me back and how can I upgrade those?

20.00

date:

| Old Habit > | New Habit > | New Actions > | New Affirmation / Mantra |

My goals for the next week

My mantra for this week is
....

Weekly Planner

4 Major Goals I'm Focused On This Week

1.
2.
3.
4.

Projects & appointments for this week	Target date	Actions for this week	Target date
monday			
tuesday			
wednesday			
thursday			
friday			
saturday			
sunday			

dream space

....
....
....

Today I would love....

Today I AM so grateful for...

My top 3 inspired actions for today are...

1.
2.
3.

My intentions for today are...

I AM
I AM
I AM
I AM

What was great about today?

What did I learn today?

After today, what behaviour do I want to upgrade?

What strengths did I use today?

date:

reminders

....
....
....
....
....
....
....
....

☐ **M & V** meditation & visualisation   ☐ **I** inspiration
☐ **E** exercise   ☐ ....

6.00
7.00
8.00
9.00
10.00
11.00
12.00
13.00
14.00
15.00
16.00
17.00
18.00
19.00
20.00

I AM in love with life

creative space

....
....
....

What if (insert possibility)....

Appreciation & Gratitude list...

M & V
meditation & visualisation

I
inspiration

E
exercise

Today, I AM most inspired to do these actions...

1.
2.
3.

6.00
7.00
8.00

The mindset I wish to create today is...

I AM
I AM
I AM
I AM

9.00
10.00
11.00
12.00

What did I enjoy about today?

13.00
14.00
15.00

What challenged me today that I can grow from?

16.00
17.00

What would I like to create instead?

18.00
19.00

What did I do really well today?

20.00

date:

ideas space

....
....
....

Today I accept that....

The things I AM grateful for in my life are...

Today, I would love to do these actions...

1.
2.
3.

Today I AM focusing on being...

I AM
I AM
I AM
I AM

What went well today?

What could I have handled differently today?

How can I open up to new ways of doing things?

What am I proud of about today?

date:

reminders

....
....
....
....
....
....

☐ **M & V** meditation & visualisation   ☐ **I** inspiration
☐ **E** exercise   ☐ ....

6.00
7.00
8.00
9.00
10.00
11.00
12.00
13.00
14.00
15.00
16.00
17.00
18.00
19.00
20.00

thoughts space

....

....

....

Today I AM going to create...

Gratitude is Wisdom...

☐ **M & V**
  meditation & visualisation

☐ **I**
  inspiration

☐ **E**
  exercise

☐ ....

Today, I feel inspired to do...

1.
2.
3.

I create my day with my thoughts, therefore...

I AM
I AM
I AM
I AM

What did I love about today?

In what area would I like to grow?

What would I like to let go of?

How did I show leadership today?

- 6.00
- 7.00
- 8.00
- 9.00
- 10.00
- 11.00
- 12.00
- 13.00
- 14.00
- 15.00
- 16.00
- 17.00
- 18.00
- 19.00
- 20.00

date:

open space

....
....
....

Today I AM going to enjoy...

When I AM grateful I open up to more...

What would I do today, if it was my last?

1.
2.
3.

Today...

I AM
I AM
I AM
I AM

What was interesting about today?

What habit would I like to develop after today?

What beliefs would I like to upgrade?

What strengths did I use today?

date:

reminders

....
....
....
....
....
....
....

☐ **M & V** meditation & visualisation   ☐ **I** inspiration
☐ **E** exercise   ☐ ....

6.00
7.00
8.00
9.00
10.00
11.00
12.00
13.00
14.00
15.00
16.00
17.00
18.00
19.00
20.00

invention space

....
....
....
....

....
....
....
....

Today is my opportunity to...

Today, I give thanks for...

☐ **M & V** meditation & visualisation   ☐ **I** inspiration
☐ **E** exercise   ☐ ....

My inspired actions for today are...

1.
2.
3.

Today I honor how I feel and...

I AM
I AM
I AM
I AM

.... 6.00
.... 7.00
.... 8.00
.... 9.00
.... 10.00
.... 11.00
.... 12.00
.... 13.00
.... 14.00
.... 15.00
.... 16.00
.... 17.00
.... 18.00
.... 19.00
.... 20.00

What was fun about today?

What was today's lesson?

What new behaviour can I adopt into my life?

What did I succeed at...

date:

My week in review

Weekly Check-in

What have I achieved this week?

What's working and why is it working?

What's not working and what am I willing to do about it?

What is one thing I can do next week that will create the biggest results in my life?

What do I need to make a decision about?

Have I had fun this week? How can I have more fun?

GET SOME ALTITUDE Where is my current attitude on a scale from 1-10? How can I get some more altitude and upgrade my attitude?

What beliefs are holding me back and how can I upgrade those?

date:

- ☐ Review Greatness Blueprint
- ☐ Review Purpose Statement
- ☐ Update 90 Day Planner
- ☐ Add Actions To Weekly Planner
- ☐ Plan Your Week

8.00
9.00
10.00
11.00
12.00
13.00
14.00
15.00
16.00
17.00
18.00
19.00
20.00

Old Habit >	New Habit >	New Actions >	New Affirmation / Mantra

My goals for the next week

My mantra for this week is ....

Weekly Planner

4 Major Goals I'm Focused On This Week

| 1. | 2. | 3. | 4. |

Projects & appointments for this week	Target date	Actions for this week	Target date
monday			
tuesday			
wednesday			
thursday			
friday			
saturday			
sunday			

fun space

....
....
....

Today I AM open to the possibility of...

What I love about my work is...

Today I AM inspired to take these actions...

1.
2.
3.

I have a winning mindset and...

I AM
I AM
I AM
I AM

What have I learned today?

How was my mindset today?

What new habit do I want to adopt into my life?

How did I give value today?

date:

reminders

....
....
....
....
....
....
....
....

☐ **M & V** meditation & visualisation   ☐ **I** inspiration
☐ **E** exercise   ☐ ....

6.00
7.00
8.00
9.00
10.00
11.00
12.00
13.00
14.00
15.00
16.00
17.00
18.00
19.00
20.00

genius space

....
....
....

Today, it would be fun to...

I AM so grateful for the simple things like...

What is the best course of action to take today?

1.
2.
3.

Today I AM creative and...

I AM
I AM
I AM
I AM

What was fantastic about today?

What skill can I develop further?

What new mindset do I want to adopt into my life?

What did I do really well today?

M & V meditation & visualisation

I inspiration

E exercise

- 6.00
- 7.00
- 8.00
- 9.00
- 10.00
- 11.00
- 12.00
- 13.00
- 14.00
- 15.00
- 16.00
- 17.00
- 18.00
- 19.00
- 20.00

date:

dream space

....
....
....

Today I would love....

Today I AM so grateful for...

My top 3 inspired actions for today are...

1.
2.
3.

My intentions for today are...

I AM
I AM
I AM
I AM

What was great about today?

What did I learn today?

After today, what behaviour do I want to upgrade?

What strengths did I use today?

date:

reminders

....
....
....
....
....
....

☐ **M & V** meditation & visualisation   ☐ **I** inspiration
☐ **E** exercise   ☐ ....

6.00 ....
7.00 ....
8.00 ....
9.00 ....
10.00 ....
11.00 ....
12.00 ....
13.00 ....
14.00 ....
15.00 ....
16.00 ....
17.00 ....
18.00 ....
19.00 ....
20.00 ....

creative space

....

....

....

What if (insert possibility)....

Appreciation & Gratitude list...

☐ M & V
meditation & visualisation

☐ I
inspiration

☐ E
exercise

....

Today, I AM most inspired to do these actions...

1.
2.
3.

The mindset I wish to create today is...

I AM
I AM
I AM
I AM

What did I enjoy about today?

What challenged me today that I can grow from?

What would I like to create instead?

What did I do really well today?

....

6.00
7.00
8.00
9.00
10.00
11.00
12.00
13.00
14.00
15.00
16.00
17.00
18.00
19.00
20.00

date:

ideas space

....
....
....

Today I accept that....

The things I AM grateful for in my life are...

Today, I would love to do these actions...

1.
2.
3.

Today I AM focusing on being...

I AM
I AM
I AM
I AM

What went well today?

What could I have handled differently today?

How can I open up to new ways of doing things?

What am I proud of about today?

date:

reminders

....
....
....
....
....
....

☐ **M & V** meditation & visualisation   ☐ **I** inspiration
☐ **E** exercise   ☐ ....

6.00
7.00
8.00
9.00
10.00
11.00
12.00
13.00
14.00
15.00
16.00
17.00
18.00
19.00
20.00

thoughts space

....
....
....

....
....
....   Today I AM going to create...
....
....
....
....   Gratitude is Wisdom...
....

☐ **M & V** meditation & visualisation   ☐ **I** inspiration
☐ **E** exercise   ☐ ....

Today, I feel inspired to do...

1.
2.
3.

6.00
7.00
8.00   I create my day with my thoughts, therefore...
9.00   I AM
10.00   I AM
11.00   I AM
           I AM
12.00
13.00   What did I love about today?
14.00
15.00   In what area would I like to grow?
16.00
17.00   What would I like to let go of?
18.00
19.00   How did I show leadership today?
20.00

date:

My week in review

Weekly Check-in

What projects have I completed this week?

☐ Review Greatness Blueprint

☐ Review Purpose Statement

What's going well and why is it?

☐ Update 90 Day Planner

☐ Add Actions To Weekly Planner

☐ Plan Your Week

What's most challenging and how can I turn it into an opportunity?

What is one thing I can do next week that will create the biggest results in my life?

What am I happy about right now?

How am I using my time? How can I prioritise better?

GET SOME ALTITUDE Where is my current attitude on a scale from 1-10? How can I get some more altitude and upgrade my attitude?

What fears are holding me back and how can I overcome those?

date:

| 8.00 |
| 9.00 |
| 10.00 |
| 11.00 |
| 12.00 |
| 13.00 |
| 14.00 |
| 15.00 |
| 16.00 |
| 17.00 |
| 18.00 |
| 19.00 |
| 20.00 |

| Old Habit > | New Habit > | New Actions > | New Affirmation / Mantra |

My goals for the next week

My mantra for this week is ....

Weekly Planner

4 Major Goals I'm Focused On This Week

| 1. | 2. | 3. | 4. |

| Projects & appointments for this week | Target date | Actions for this week | Target date |

monday

tuesday

wednesday

thursday

friday

saturday

sunday

open space

....
....
....

Today I AM going to enjoy...

When I AM grateful I open up to more...

What would I do today, if it was my last?
1.
2.
3.

Today...
I AM
I AM
I AM
I AM

What was interesting about today?

What habit would I like to develop after today?

What beliefs would I like to upgrade?

What strengths did I use today?

date:

reminders

....
....
....
....
....
....
....

☐ **M & V** meditation & visualisation   ☐ **I** inspiration
☐ **E** exercise

6.00
7.00
8.00
9.00
10.00
11.00
12.00
13.00
14.00
15.00
16.00
17.00
18.00
19.00
20.00

invention space

....
....
....

Today is my opportunity to...

Today, I give thanks for...

My inspired actions for today are...

1.
2.
3.

Today I honor how I feel and...

I AM
I AM
I AM
I AM

What was fun about today?

What was today's lesson?

What new behaviour can I adopt into my life?

What did I succeed at...

M & V
meditation & visualisation

I
inspiration

E
exercise

6.00
7.00
8.00
9.00
10.00
11.00
12.00
13.00
14.00
15.00
16.00
17.00
18.00
19.00
20.00

date:

fun space

....
....
....

Today I AM open to the possibility of...

What I love about my work is...

Today I AM inspired to take these actions...

1.
2.
3.

I have a winning mindset and...

I AM
I AM
I AM
I AM

What have I learned today?

How was my mindset today?

What new habit do I want to adopt into my life?

How did I give value today?

date:

reminders

....
....
....
....
....
....
....

☐ **M & V** meditation & visualisation ☐ **I** inspiration
☐ **E** exercise ☐ ....

6.00
7.00
8.00
9.00
10.00
11.00
12.00
13.00
14.00
15.00
16.00
17.00
18.00
19.00
20.00

genius space

....
....
....

Today, it would be fun to...

I AM so grateful for the simple things like...

M & V
meditation & visualisation

E
exercise

☐ **I**
inspiration

☐ ....

What is the best course of action to take today?

1.
2.
3.

Today I AM creative and...

I AM
I AM
I AM
I AM

What was fantastic about today?

What skill can I develop further?

What new mindset do I want to adopt into my life?

What did I do really well today?

6.00
7.00
8.00
9.00
10.00
11.00
12.00
13.00
14.00
15.00
16.00
17.00
18.00
19.00
20.00

date:

dream space

....
....
....

Today I would love....

Today I AM so grateful for...

My top 3 inspired actions for today are...

1.
2.
3.

My intentions for today are...

I AM
I AM
I AM
I AM

date:

What was great about today?

What did I learn today?

After today, what behaviour do I want to upgrade?

What strengths did I use today?

reminders

....
....
....
....
....
....
....

☐ **M & V** meditation & visualisation   ☐ **I** inspiration
☐ **E** exercise   ☐ ....

I AM peaceful

6.00
7.00
8.00
9.00
10.00
11.00
12.00
13.00
14.00
15.00
16.00
17.00
18.00
19.00
20.00

creative space

....
....
....

What if (insert possibility)....

Appreciation & Gratitude list...

M & V meditation & visualisation
I inspiration
E exercise

Today, I AM most inspired to do these actions...

1.
2.
3.

The mindset I wish to create today is...

I AM
I AM
I AM
I AM

6.00
7.00
8.00
9.00
10.00
11.00

What did I enjoy about today?

12.00
13.00
14.00

What challenged me today that I can grow from?

15.00
16.00

What would I like to create instead?

17.00
18.00
19.00

What did I do really well today?

20.00

date:

My week in review

Weekly Check-in

What have I achieved on my greatness blueprint this week?

- [ ] Review Greatness Blueprint
- [ ] Review Purpose Statement
- [ ] Update 90 Day Planner
- [ ] Add Actions To Weekly Planner
- [ ] Plan Your Week

Where am I seeing the desired results & why?

What do I need to start or stop?

What is one thing I can do next week that will create the biggest results in my life?

Where can I be a better leader?

Do I need to upgrade my communication skills? How can I be better?

GET SOME ALTITUDE Where is my current attitude on a scale from 1-10? How can I get some more altitude and upgrade my attitude?

What negative attitudes are holding me back and how can I overcome those?

date:

8.00
9.00
10.00
11.00
12.00
13.00
14.00
15.00
16.00
17.00
18.00
19.00
20.00

Old Habit >	New Habit >	New Actions >	New Affirmation / Mantra

My goals for the next week

My mantra for this week is ....

Weekly Planner

4 Major Goals I'm Focused On This Week

| 1. | 2. | 3. | 4. |

| Projects & appointments for this week | Target date | Actions for this week | Target date |

monday

tuesday

wednesday

thursday

friday

saturday

sunday

ideas space

....

....

....

Today I accept that....

The things I AM grateful for in my life are...

Today, I would love to do these actions...

1.
2.
3.

Today I AM focusing on being...

I AM

I AM

I AM

I AM

What went well today?

What could I have handled differently today?

How can I open up to new ways of doing things?

What am I proud of about today?

date:

reminders

....

....

....

....

....

....

....

☐ **M & V** meditation & visualisation ☐ **I** inspiration

☐ **E** exercise ☐ ....

6.00
7.00
8.00
9.00
10.00
11.00
12.00
13.00
14.00
15.00
16.00
17.00
18.00
19.00
20.00

thoughts space

....
....
....

Today I AM going to create...

Gratitude is Wisdom...

M & V meditation & visualisation
I inspiration
E exercise

Today, I feel inspired to do...

1.
2.
3.

6.00
7.00
8.00

I create my day with my thoughts, therefore...

I AM
I AM
I AM
I AM

9.00
10.00
11.00
12.00

What did I love about today?

13.00
14.00

In what area would I like to grow?

15.00
16.00

What would I like to let go of?

17.00
18.00

How did I show leadership today?

19.00
20.00

date:

open space

....
....
....

Today I AM going to enjoy...

When I AM grateful I open up to more...

What would I do today, if it was my last?

1.
2.
3.

Today...
I AM
I AM
I AM
I AM

What was interesting about today?

What habit would I like to develop after today?

What beliefs would I like to upgrade?

What strengths did I use today?

date:

reminders

....
....
....
....
....
....
....

☐ **M & V** meditation & visualisation   ☐ **I** inspiration
☐ **E** exercise   ☐ ....

6.00
7.00
8.00
9.00
10.00
11.00
12.00
13.00
14.00
15.00
16.00
17.00
18.00
19.00
20.00

invention space

....
....
....

Today is my opportunity to...

Today, I give thanks for...

My inspired actions for today are...

1.
2.
3.

Today I honor how I feel and...

I AM
I AM
I AM
I AM

What was fun about today?

What was today's lesson?

What new behaviour can I adopt into my life?

What did I succeed at...

M & V — meditation & visualisation
E — exercise
I — inspiration
....

6.00
7.00
8.00
9.00
10.00
11.00
12.00
13.00
14.00
15.00
16.00
17.00
18.00
19.00
20.00

date:

fun space

....
....
....

Today I AM open to the possibility of...

What I love about my work is...

Today I AM inspired to take these actions...

1.
2.
3.

I have a winning mindset and...

I AM
I AM
I AM
I AM

What have I learned today?

How was my mindset today?

What new habit do I want to adopt into my life?

How did I give value today?

date:

reminders

....
....
....
....
....
....
....
....

☐ **M & V** meditation & visualisation   ☐ **I** inspiration
☐ **E** exercise

6.00
7.00
8.00
9.00
10.00
11.00
12.00
13.00
14.00
15.00
16.00
17.00
18.00
19.00
20.00

genius space

....
....
....

Today, it would be fun to...

I AM so grateful for the simple things like...

M & V
meditation & visualisation

I
inspiration

E
exercise

What is the best course of action to take today?

1.
2.
3.

Today I AM creative and...

I AM
I AM
I AM
I AM

What was fantastic about today?

What skill can I develop further?

What new mindset do I want to adopt into my life?

What did I do really well today?

6.00
7.00
8.00
9.00
10.00
11.00
12.00
13.00
14.00
15.00
16.00
17.00
18.00
19.00
20.00

date:

My week in review

Weekly Check-in

What major goals have I achieved this month?

☐ Review Greatness Blueprint

☐ Review Purpose Statement

Where am I having success and why?

☐ Update 90 Day Planner

☐ Add Actions To Weekly Planner

☐ Plan Your Week

What are the biggest distractions in my life and how can I remove them?

8.00

9.00

What is one thing I can do next week that will create the biggest results in my life?

10.00

11.00

What am I committed to achieving in my life right now?

12.00

13.00

14.00

What is my home and work environment like? Does it inspire me?

15.00

16.00

GET SOME ALTITUDE Where is my current attitude on a scale from 1-10? How can I get some more altitude and upgrade my attitude?

17.00

18.00

What disempowering thoughts are holding me back and how can I upgrade those?

19.00

20.00

date:

| Old Habit > | New Habit > | New Actions > | New Affirmation / Mantra |

My goals for the next week

Weekly Planner

My mantra for this week is ....

4 Major Goals I'm Focused On This Week

| 1. | 2. | 3. | 4. |

| Projects & appointments for this week | Target date | Actions for this week | Target date |

- monday
- tuesday
- wednesday
- thursday
- friday
- saturday
- sunday

dream space

....
....
....

Today I would love....

Today I AM so grateful for...

My top 3 inspired actions for today are...

1.
2.
3.

My intentions for today are...

I AM
I AM
I AM
I AM

What was great about today?

What did I learn today?

After today, what behaviour do I want to upgrade?

What strengths did I use today?

date:

reminders

....
....
....
....
....
....
....

☐ **M & V** meditation & visualisation   ☐ **I** inspiration
☐ **E** exercise

6.00
7.00
8.00
9.00
10.00
11.00
12.00
13.00
14.00
15.00
16.00
17.00
18.00
19.00
20.00

creative space

....
....
....

What if (insert possibility)....

Appreciation & Gratitude list...

Today, I AM most inspired to do these actions...

1.
2.
3.

The mindset I wish to create today is...

I AM
I AM
I AM
I AM

What did I enjoy about today?

What challenged me today that I can grow from?

What would I like to create instead?

What did I do really well today?

M & V
meditation & visualisation

E
exercise

I
inspiration

6.00
7.00
8.00
9.00
10.00
11.00
12.00
13.00
14.00
15.00
16.00
17.00
18.00
19.00
20.00

date:

I AM in love with life

ideas space

....

....

....

Today I accept that....

The things I AM grateful for in my life are...

Today, I would love to do these actions...

1.
2.
3.

Today I AM focusing on being...

I AM
I AM
I AM
I AM

What went well today?

What could I have handled differently today?

How can I open up to new ways of doing things?

What am I proud of about today?

date:

reminders

....

....

....

....

....

....

....

....

☐ **M & V** meditation & visualisation   ☐ **I** inspiration

☐ **E** exercise   ☐ ....

6.00
7.00
8.00
9.00
10.00
11.00
12.00
13.00
14.00
15.00
16.00
17.00
18.00
19.00
20.00

thoughts space

....
....
....

Today I AM going to create...

....
....
....
....
....
....
....

Gratitude is Wisdom...

M & V
meditation & visualisation

I
inspiration

E
exercise ....

Today, I feel inspired to do...

1.
2.
3.

6.00
7.00
8.00

I create my day with my thoughts, therefore...

I AM
I AM
I AM
I AM

9.00
10.00
11.00
12.00

What did I love about today?

13.00
14.00

In what area would I like to grow?

15.00
16.00

What would I like to let go of?

17.00
18.00

How did I show leadership today?

19.00
20.00

date:

open space

....
....
....

Today I AM going to enjoy...

When I AM grateful I open up to more...

What would I do today, if it was my last?

1.
2.
3.

Today...
I AM
I AM
I AM
I AM

What was interesting about today?

What habit would I like to develop after today?

What beliefs would I like to upgrade?

What strengths did I use today?

date:

reminders

....
....
....
....
....
....
....

☐ **M & V** meditation & visualisation   ☐ **I** inspiration
☐ **E** exercise   ☐ ....

6.00
7.00
8.00
9.00
10.00
11.00
12.00
13.00
14.00
15.00
16.00
17.00
18.00
19.00
20.00

invention space

....
....
....

Today is my opportunity to...

Today, I give thanks for...

M & V meditation & visualisation
I inspiration
E exercise

My inspired actions for today are...

1.
2.
3.

6.00
7.00
8.00
9.00
10.00
11.00

Today I honor how I feel and...

I AM
I AM
I AM
I AM

12.00
13.00

What was fun about today?

14.00
15.00

What was today's lesson?

16.00
17.00

What new behaviour can I adopt into my life?

18.00
19.00

What did I succeed at...

20.00

date:

My week in review

Weekly Check-in

What have I achieved this week?

☐ Review Greatness Blueprint

☐ Review Purpose Statement

☐ Update 90 Day Planner

What's working and why is it working?

☐ Add Actions To Weekly Planner

☐ Plan Your Week

What's not working and what am I willing to do about it?

8.00

9.00

What is one thing I can do next week that will create the biggest results in my life?

10.00

11.00

12.00

What do I need to make a decision about?

13.00

14.00

date:

Have I had fun this week? How can I have more fun?

15.00

16.00

17.00

GET SOME ALTITUDE Where is my current attitude on a scale from 1 -10? How can I get some more altitude and upgrade my attitude?

18.00

19.00

What beliefs are holding me back and how can I upgrade those?

20.00

Old Habit >	New Habit >	New Actions >	New Affirmation / Mantra

My goals for the next week

Weekly Planner

My mantra for this week is ....

4 Major Goals I'm Focused On This Week

1.	2.	3.	4.

Projects & appointments for this week	Target date	Actions for this week	Target date
monday			
tuesday			
wednesday			
thursday			
friday			
saturday			
sunday			

fun space

....

....

....

Today I AM open to the possibility of...

What I love about my work is...

Today I AM inspired to take these actions...

1.
2.
3.

I have a winning mindset and...

I AM

I AM

I AM

I AM

What have I learned today?

How was my mindset today?

What new habit do I want to adopt into my life?

How did I give value today?

date:

reminders

....

....

....

....

....

....

....

☐ **M & V** meditation & visualisation ☐ **I** inspiration
☐ **E** exercise ☐ ....

6.00
7.00
8.00
9.00
10.00
11.00
12.00
13.00
14.00
15.00
16.00
17.00
18.00
19.00
20.00

genius space

....
....
....

Today, it would be fun to...

I AM so grateful for the simple things like...

What is the best course of action to take today?

1.
2.
3.

Today I AM creative and...

I AM
I AM
I AM
I AM

What was fantastic about today?

What skill can I develop further?

What new mindset do I want to adopt into my life?

What did I do really well today?

M & V meditation & visualisation
I inspiration
E exercise

6.00
7.00
8.00
9.00
10.00
11.00
12.00
13.00
14.00
15.00
16.00
17.00
18.00
19.00
20.00

date:

dream space

....
....
....

Today I would love....

Today I AM so grateful for...

My top 3 inspired actions for today are...

1.
2.
3.

My intentions for today are...

I AM
I AM
I AM
I AM

What was great about today?

What did I learn today?

After today, what behaviour do I want to upgrade?

What strengths did I use today?

date:

reminders

....
....
....
....
....
....
....

☐ **M & V** meditation & visualisation ☐ **I** inspiration
☐ **E** exercise ☐ ....

6.00
7.00
8.00
9.00
10.00
11.00
12.00
13.00
14.00
15.00
16.00
17.00
18.00
19.00
20.00

creative space

....
....
....
.... What if (insert possibility)....
....
....
.... Appreciation & Gratitude list...
....

☐ **M & V** meditation & visualisation   ☐ **I** inspiration
☐ **E** exercise   ☐ ....

Today, I AM most inspired to do these actions...

1.
2.
3.

6.00
7.00
8.00

The mindset I wish to create today is...

9.00

I AM

10.00

I AM
I AM

11.00

I AM

12.00

What did I enjoy about today?

13.00

14.00

What challenged me today that I can grow from?

15.00

16.00

What would I like to create instead?

17.00

18.00

19.00

What did I do really well today?

20.00

date:

ideas space

....
....
....

Today I accept that....

The things I AM grateful for in my life are...

Today, I would love to do these actions...

1.
2.
3.

Today I AM focusing on being...

I AM
I AM
I AM
I AM

What went well today?

What could I have handled differently today?

How can I open up to new ways of doing things?

What am I proud of about today?

date:

reminders

....
....
....
....
....
....
....

☐ **M & V** meditation & visualisation ☐ **I** inspiration
☐ **E** exercise ☐ ....

6.00
7.00
8.00
9.00
10.00
11.00
12.00
13.00
14.00
15.00
16.00
17.00
18.00
19.00
20.00

thoughts space

....
....
....

Today I AM going to create...

....
....
....
....
....
....
....

Gratitude is Wisdom...

☐ **M & V**
    meditation & visualisation
☐ **I**
    inspiration
☐ **E**
    exercise   ....

Today, I feel inspired to do...

1.
2.
3.

6.00
7.00
8.00

I create my day with my thoughts, therefore...

I AM
I AM
I AM
I AM

9.00
10.00
11.00
12.00

What did I love about today?

13.00
14.00

In what area would I like to grow?

15.00
16.00

What would I like to let go of?

17.00
18.00

How did I show leadership today?

19.00
20.00

date:

My week in review

Weekly Check-in

What projects have I completed this week?

☐ Review Greatness Blueprint

☐ Review Purpose Statement

What's going well and why is it?

☐ Update 90 Day Planner

☐ Add Actions To Weekly Planner

☐ Plan Your Week

What's most challenging and how can I turn it into an opportunity?

What is one thing I can do next week that will create the biggest results in my life?

8.00

9.00

10.00

11.00

What am I happy about right now?

12.00

13.00

14.00

date:

How am I using my time? How can I prioritise better?

15.00

16.00

GET SOME ALTITUDE Where is my current attitude on a scale from 1-10? How can I get some more altitude and upgrade my attitude?

17.00

18.00

19.00

What fears are holding me back and how can I overcome those?

20.00

Old Habit > | New Habit > | New Actions > | New Affirmation / Mantra

My goals for the next week

Weekly Planner

My mantra for this week is ....

4 Major Goals I'm Focused On This Week

| 1. | 2. | 3. | 4. |

Projects & appointments for this week	Target date	Actions for this week	Target date
monday			
tuesday			
wednesday			
thursday			
friday			
saturday			
sunday			

open space

....
....
....

Today I AM going to enjoy...

When I AM grateful I open up to more...

What would I do today, if it was my last?

1.
2.
3.

Today...

I AM
I AM
I AM
I AM

What was interesting about today?

What habit would I like to develop after today?

What beliefs would I like to upgrade?

What strengths did I use today?

date:

reminders

....
....
....
....
....
....

☐ **M & V** meditation & visualisation   ☐ **I** inspiration
☐ **E** exercise   ☐ ....

6.00
7.00
8.00
9.00
10.00
11.00
12.00
13.00
14.00
15.00
16.00
17.00
18.00
19.00
20.00

invention space

....
....
....

Today is my opportunity to...

Today, I give thanks for...

My inspired actions for today are...

1.
2.
3.

Today I honor how I feel and...

I AM
I AM
I AM
I AM

What was fun about today?

What was today's lesson?

What new behaviour can I adopt into my life?

What did I succeed at...

M & V meditation & visualisation
I inspiration
E exercise

6.00	
7.00	
8.00	
9.00	
10.00	
11.00	
12.00	
13.00	
14.00	
15.00	
16.00	
17.00	
18.00	
19.00	
20.00	

date:

fun space

....
....
....

Today I AM open to the possibility of...

What I love about my work is...

Today I AM inspired to take these actions...

1.
2.
3.

I have a winning mindset and...

I AM
I AM
I AM
I AM

What have I learned today?

How was my mindset today?

What new habit do I want to adopt into my life?

How did I give value today?

date:

reminders

....
....
....
....
....
....

☐ **M & V** meditation & visualisation   ☐ **I** inspiration
☐ **E** exercise   ☐ ....

6.00
7.00
8.00
9.00
10.00
11.00
12.00
13.00
14.00
15.00
16.00
17.00
18.00
19.00
20.00

genius space

....
....
....

Today, it would be fun to...

I AM so grateful for the simple things like...

M & V
meditation & visualisation

I
inspiration

E
exercise

What is the best course of action to take today?

1.
2.
3.

Today I AM creative and...

I AM
I AM
I AM
I AM

What was fantastic about today?

What skill can I develop further?

What new mindset do I want to adopt into my life?

What did I do really well today?

6.00
7.00
8.00
9.00
10.00
11.00
12.00
13.00
14.00
15.00
16.00
17.00
18.00
19.00
20.00

date:

dream space

....
....
....

Today I would love....

Today I AM so grateful for...

My top 3 inspired actions for today are...

1.
2.
3.

My intentions for today are...

I AM
I AM
I AM
I AM

What was great about today?

What did I learn today?

After today, what behaviour do I want to upgrade?

What strengths did I use today?

date:

reminders

....
....
....
....
....
....
....

☐ **M & V** meditation & visualisation   ☐ **I** inspiration
☐ **E** exercise   ☐ ....

6.00 ....
7.00 ....
8.00 ....
9.00 ....
10.00 ....
11.00 ....
12.00 ....
13.00 ....
14.00 ....
15.00 ....
16.00 ....
17.00 ....
18.00 ....
19.00 ....
20.00 ....

creative space

....
....
....
....
.... What if (insert possibility)....
....
....
....
....
.... Appreciation & Gratitude list...
....

M & V meditation & visualisation   **I** inspiration
E exercise   ....

Today, I AM most inspired to do these actions...

1.
2.
3.

The mindset I wish to create today is...

I AM
I AM
I AM
I AM

I AM peaceful

6.00
7.00
8.00
9.00
10.00
11.00
12.00   What did I enjoy about today?
13.00
14.00   What challenged me today that I can grow from?
15.00
16.00
17.00   What would I like to create instead?
18.00
19.00   What did I do really well today?
20.00

date:

My week in review

Weekly Check-in

What have I achieved on my greatness blueprint this week?

☐ Review Greatness Blueprint

☐ Review Purpose Statement

Where am I seeing the desired results & why?

☐ Update 90 Day Planner

☐ Add Actions To Weekly Planner

☐ Plan Your Week

What do I need to start or stop?

8.00

9.00

What is one thing I can do next week that will create the biggest results in my life?

10.00

11.00

Where can I be a better leader?

12.00

13.00

date:

14.00

Do I need to upgrade my communication skills? How can I be better?

15.00

16.00

17.00

GET SOME ALTITUDE Where is my current attitude on a scale from 1-10? How can I get some more altitude and upgrade my attitude?

18.00

19.00

What negative attitudes are holding me back and how can I overcome those?

20.00

| Old Habit > | New Habit > | New Actions > | New Affirmation / Mantra |

My goals for the next week

Weekly Planner

My mantra for this week is ....

4 Major Goals I'm Focused On This Week

| 1. | 2. | 3. | 4. |

| Projects & appointments for this week | Target date | Actions for this week | Target date |

- monday
- tuesday
- wednesday
- thursday
- friday
- saturday
- sunday

ideas space

....
....
....

Today I accept that....

The things I AM grateful for in my life are...

Today, I would love to do these actions...

1.
2.
3.

Today I AM focusing on being...

I AM
I AM
I AM
I AM

What went well today?

What could I have handled differently today?

How can I open up to new ways of doing things?

What am I proud of about today?

date:

reminders

....
....
....
....
....
....
....
....

☐ **M & V** meditation & visualisation ☐ **I** inspiration
☐ **E** exercise ☐ ....

6.00
7.00
8.00
9.00
10.00
11.00
12.00
13.00
14.00
15.00
16.00
17.00
18.00
19.00
20.00

thoughts space

....

....

....

Today I AM going to create...

Gratitude is Wisdom...

M & V meditation & visualisation

I inspiration

E exercise

....

Today, I feel inspired to do...

1.
2.
3.

I create my day with my thoughts, therefore...

I AM
I AM
I AM
I AM

What did I love about today?

In what area would I like to grow?

What would I like to let go of?

How did I show leadership today?

6.00
7.00
8.00
9.00
10.00
11.00
12.00
13.00
14.00
15.00
16.00
17.00
18.00
19.00
20.00

date:

open space

....

....

....

Today I AM going to enjoy...

When I AM grateful I open up to more...

What would I do today, if it was my last?
1.
2.
3.

Today...
I AM
I AM
I AM
I AM

What was interesting about today?

What habit would I like to develop after today?

What beliefs would I like to upgrade?

What strengths did I use today?

date:

reminders

....

....

....

....

....

....

☐ **M & V** meditation & visualisation   ☐ **I** inspiration
☐ **E** exercise   ☐ ....

6.00
7.00
8.00
9.00
10.00
11.00
12.00
13.00
14.00
15.00
16.00
17.00
18.00
19.00
20.00

invention space

....
....
....

Today is my opportunity to...

Today, I give thanks for...

My inspired actions for today are...

1.
2.
3.

Today I honor how I feel and...

I AM
I AM
I AM
I AM

What was fun about today?

What was today's lesson?

What new behaviour can I adopt into my life?

What did I succeed at...

....
....
....
....
....
....
....
....

M & V — meditation & visualisation
I — inspiration
E — exercise

- 6.00
- 7.00
- 8.00
- 9.00
- 10.00
- 11.00
- 12.00
- 13.00
- 14.00
- 15.00
- 16.00
- 17.00
- 18.00
- 19.00
- 20.00

date:

fun space

....
....
....

Today I AM open to the possibility of...

What I love about my work is...

Today I AM inspired to take these actions...

1.
2.
3.

I have a winning mindset and...

I AM
I AM
I AM
I AM

What have I learned today?

How was my mindset today?

What new habit do I want to adopt into my life?

How did I give value today?

date:

reminders

....
....
....
....
....
||||||||||||||||||||||||||||||||||||||||||||||||||
....
||||||||||||||||||||||||||||||

☐ **M & V** meditation & visualisation ☐ **I** inspiration
☐ **E** exercise ☐ ....

6.00
7.00
8.00
9.00
10.00
11.00
12.00
13.00
14.00
15.00
16.00
17.00
18.00
19.00
20.00

genius space

....
....
....

Today, it would be fun to...

I AM so grateful for the simple things like...

☐ M & V
  meditation & visualisation
☐ I
  inspiration
☐ E
  exercise
....

What is the best course of action to take today?

1.
2.
3.

Today I AM creative and...

I AM
I AM
I AM
I AM

What was fantastic about today?

What skill can I develop further?

What new mindset do I want to adopt into my life?

What did I do really well today?

....
....
....
....
....
....
....
....

6.00
7.00
8.00
9.00
10.00
11.00
12.00
13.00
14.00
15.00
16.00
17.00
18.00
19.00
20.00

date:

My week in review

Weekly Check-in

What major goals have I achieved this month?

☐ Review Greatness Blueprint

☐ Review Purpose Statement

Where am I having success and why?

☐ Update 90 Day Planner

☐ Add Actions To Weekly Planner

☐ Plan Your Week

What are the biggest distractions in my life and how can I remove them?

8.00

9.00

What is one thing I can do next week that will create the biggest results in my life?

10.00

11.00

What am I committed to achieving in my life right now?

12.00

13.00

14.00

What is my home and work environment like? Does it inspire me?

15.00

16.00

GET SOME ALTITUDE Where is my current attitude on a scale from 1-10? How can I get some more altitude and upgrade my attitude?

17.00

18.00

19.00

What disempowering thoughts are holding me back and how can I upgrade those?

20.00

date:

Old Habit >	New Habit >	New Actions >	New Affirmation / Mantra

My goals for the next week

Weekly Planner

My mantra for this week is ....

4 Major Goals I'm Focused On This Week

| 1. | 2. | 3. | 4. |

| Projects & appointments for this week | Target date | Actions for this week | Target date |

monday

tuesday

wednesday

thursday

friday

saturday

sunday

ideas space

....

....

....

Today I accept that....

The things I AM grateful for in my life are...

Today, I would love to do these actions...

1.
2.
3.

Today I AM focusing on being...

I AM
I AM
I AM
I AM

What went well today?

What could I have handled differently today?

How can I open up to new ways of doing things?

What am I proud of about today?

date:

reminders

....

....

....

....

....

....

....

☐ **M & V** meditation & visualisation   ☐ **I** inspiration
☐ **E** exercise

6.00 ....
7.00 ....
8.00 ....
9.00 ....
10.00 ....
11.00 ....
12.00 ....
13.00 ....
14.00 ....
15.00 ....
16.00 ....
17.00 ....
18.00 ....
19.00 ....
20.00 ....

thoughts space

....
....
....

Today I AM going to create...

Gratitude is Wisdom...

M & V
meditation & visualisation

I
inspiration

E
exercise

Today, I feel inspired to do...

1.
2.
3.

I create my day with my thoughts, therefore...

I AM
I AM
I AM
I AM

What did I love about today?

In what area would I like to grow?

What would I like to let go of?

How did I show leadership today?

date:

6.00
7.00
8.00
9.00
10.00
11.00
12.00
13.00
14.00
15.00
16.00
17.00
18.00
19.00
20.00

open space

....

....

....

Today I AM going to enjoy...

When I AM grateful I open up to more...

What would I do today, if it was my last?

1.
2.
3.

Today...
I AM
I AM
I AM
I AM

What was interesting about today?

What habit would I like to develop after today?

What beliefs would I like to upgrade?

What strengths did I use today?

date:

reminders

....

....

....

....

....

....

....

....

| ☐ | **M & V** meditation & visualisation | ☐ | **I** inspiration |
| ☐ | **E** exercise | ☐ | .... |

6.00 ....
7.00 ....
8.00 ....
9.00 ....
10.00 ....
11.00 ....
12.00 ....
13.00 ....
14.00 ....
15.00 ....
16.00 ....
17.00 ....
18.00 ....
19.00 ....
20.00 ....

invention space

....
....
....

Today is my opportunity to...

Today, I give thanks for...

My inspired actions for today are...

1.
2.
3.

Today I honor how I feel and...

I AM
I AM
I AM
I AM

What was fun about today?

What was today's lesson?

What new behaviour can I adopt into my life?

What did I succeed at...

M & V meditation & visualisation
I inspiration
E exercise

6.00
7.00
8.00
9.00
10.00
11.00
12.00
13.00
14.00
15.00
16.00
17.00
18.00
19.00
20.00

date:

fun space

....
....
....

Today I AM open to the possibility of...

What I love about my work is...

Today I AM inspired to take these actions...

1.
2.
3.

I have a winning mindset and...

I AM
I AM
I AM
I AM

What have I learned today?

How was my mindset today?

What new habit do I want to adopt into my life?

How did I give value today?

date:

reminders

....
....
....
....
....
....

| | M & V meditation & visualisation | | I inspiration |
| | E exercise | | .... |

6.00
7.00
8.00
9.00
10.00
11.00
12.00
13.00
14.00
15.00
16.00
17.00
18.00
19.00
20.00

genius space

....
....
....

Today, it would be fun to...

I AM so grateful for the simple things like...

....
....
....
....
....
....
....

☐ M & V
  meditation & visualisation
☐ I
  inspiration
☐ E
  exercise
☐ ....

What is the best course of action to take today?

1.
2.
3.

Today I AM creative and...

I AM
I AM
I AM
I AM

What was fantastic about today?

What skill can I develop further?

What new mindset do I want to adopt into my life?

What did I do really well today?

6.00
7.00
8.00
9.00
10.00
11.00
12.00
13.00
14.00
15.00
16.00
17.00
18.00
19.00
20.00

date:

90 Day Check-in

Welcome to your 90-day check-in! It's time to celebrate your achievements, identify what needs attention, check your life balance, and set your focus for the next 90 days. Use the answers to the questions to plan your next quarter and adjust your goals, intentions, and actions accordingly. Transfer these to Your Achievements page to keep inspired and motivated about your progress.

What major goals have I completed this past 90 days?
What am I happy about?

How can I align more with my Greatness Blueprint and overall purpose? Does my vision still inspire me or do I need to upgrade my strategy?

What would I love to create in the next 90 days?
What goal or project am I focusing on?

What new mindset do I wish to develop?
What is no longer acceptable to me?

How do I feel about the 8 areas of my life?
How can I become more balanced and happy?
What areas of my life need attention?

Am I embracing change or resisting it?
How can I open up to more expansion?

Do I have a good team of people around me?
How can I surround myself with great people?
Who is my mentor?

What else have I noticed about my life in the last 90 days?

☐ Review Greatness Blueprint ☐ Review Your Yearly Planner ☐ Plan Your Week
☐ Review Purpose Statement ☐ Complete Next 90 Day Planner ☐ Celebrate Your Progress

My goals for the next 90 days

90 Day Planner

Goal:

Project:

Target date:

Actions to complete this goal:

1.
2.
3.
4.

Why I'd love to achieve this goal:

How will I feel when I've reached this goal?

Goal:

Project:

Target date:

Actions to complete this goal:

1.
2.
3.
4.

Why I'd love to achieve this goal:

How will I feel when I've reached this goal?

Goal:

Project:

Target date:

Actions to complete this goal:

1.
2.
3.
4.

Why I'd love to achieve this goal:

How will I feel when I've reached this goal?

Goal:

Project:

Target date:

Actions to complete this goal:

1.
2.
3.
4.

Why I'd love to achieve this goal:

How will I feel when I've reached this goal?

Don't wait for extraordinary opportunities.

I am the creator of my reality!

Seize common occasions and make them great. Weak men wait for opportunities, strong men make them.

Orison Swett Marden

My Genius Space

My goals for the next week

Weekly Planner

My mantra for this week is

4 Major Goals I'm Focused On This Week

| 1. | 2. | 3. | 4. |

| Projects & appointments for this week | Target date | Actions for this week | Target date |

monday

tuesday

wednesday

thursday

friday

saturday

sunday

dream space

....
....
....

Today I would love....

Today I AM so grateful for...

My top 3 inspired actions for today are...

1.
2.
3.

My intentions for today are...

I AM
I AM
I AM
I AM

What was great about today?

What did I learn today?

After today, what behaviour do I want to upgrade?

What strengths did I use today?

date:

reminders

....
....
....
....
....
....
|||||||||||||||||||||||||||||||||||||||||
....
....

☐ **M & V** meditation & visualisation ☐ **I** inspiration
☐ **E** exercise ☐

6.00
7.00
8.00
9.00
10.00
11.00
12.00
13.00
14.00
15.00
16.00
17.00
18.00
19.00
20.00

creative space

....
....
....

What if (insert possibility)....

I AM happy

Appreciation & Gratitude list...

M & V
meditation & visualisation

I
inspiration

E
exercise

Today, I AM most inspired to do these actions...

1.
2.
3.

The mindset I wish to create today is...

I AM
I AM
I AM
I AM

6.00
7.00
8.00
9.00
10.00
11.00
12.00

What did I enjoy about today?

13.00
14.00
15.00
16.00

What challenged me today that I can grow from?

17.00
18.00

What would I like to create instead?

19.00
20.00

What did I do really well today?

date:

ideas space

....
....
....

Today I accept that....

The things I AM grateful for in my life are...

Today, I would love to do these actions...

1.
2.
3.

Today I AM focusing on being...

I AM
I AM
I AM
I AM

What went well today?

What could I have handled differently today?

How can I open up to new ways of doing things?

What am I proud of about today?

date:

reminders

....
....
....
....
....
....
....

☐ **M & V** meditation & visualisation ☐ **I** inspiration
☐ **E** exercise ☐ ....

6.00
7.00
8.00
9.00
10.00
11.00
12.00
13.00
14.00
15.00
16.00
17.00
18.00
19.00
20.00

thoughts space

....
....
....

Today I AM going to create...

Gratitude is Wisdom...

M & V meditation & visualisation
I inspiration
E exercise

Today, I feel inspired to do...

1.
2.
3.

I create my day with my thoughts, therefore...

I AM
I AM
I AM
I AM

What did I love about today?

In what area would I like to grow?

What would I like to let go of?

How did I show leadership today?

- 6.00
- 7.00
- 8.00
- 9.00
- 10.00
- 11.00
- 12.00
- 13.00
- 14.00
- 15.00
- 16.00
- 17.00
- 18.00
- 19.00
- 20.00

date:

open space

....

....

....

Today I AM going to enjoy...

When I AM grateful I open up to more...

What would I do today, if it was my last?

1.
2.
3.

Today...

I AM

I AM

I AM

I AM

What was interesting about today?

What habit would I like to develop after today?

What beliefs would I like to upgrade?

What strengths did I use today?

date:

reminders

....

....

....

....

....

....

....

....

☐ **M & V** meditation & visualisation ☐ **I** inspiration
☐ **E** exercise ☐ ....

6.00
7.00
8.00
9.00
10.00
11.00
12.00
13.00
14.00
15.00
16.00
17.00
18.00
19.00
20.00

invention space

....
....
....

Today is my opportunity to...

Today, I give thanks for...

M & V meditation & visualisation
I inspiration
E exercise

My inspired actions for today are...

1.
2.
3.

6.00
7.00
8.00
9.00
10.00
11.00

Today I honor how I feel and...

I AM
I AM
I AM
I AM

12.00
13.00
14.00

What was fun about today?

What was today's lesson?

15.00
16.00
17.00

What new behaviour can I adopt into my life?

18.00
19.00
20.00

What did I succeed at...

date:

My week in review

Weekly Check-in

What have I achieved this week?

☐ Review Greatness Blueprint

☐ Review Purpose Statement

☐ Update 90 Day Planner

What's working and why is it working?

☐ Add Actions To Weekly Planner

☐ Plan Your Week

What's not working and what am I willing to do about it?

8.00

9.00

What is one thing I can do next week that will create the biggest results in my life?

10.00

11.00

What do I need to make a decision about?

12.00

13.00

14.00

Have I had fun this week? How can I have more fun?

15.00

16.00

GET SOME ALTITUDE Where is my current attitude on a scale from 1-10? How can I get some more altitude and upgrade my attitude?

17.00

18.00

19.00

What beliefs are holding me back and how can I upgrade those?

20.00

date:

| Old Habit > | New Habit > | New Actions > | New Affirmation / Mantra |

My goals for the next week

Weekly Planner

My mantra for this week is ....

4 Major Goals I'm Focused On This Week

1.   2.   3.   4.

Projects & appointments for this week	Target date	Actions for this week	Target date

- monday
- tuesday
- wednesday
- thursday
- friday
- saturday
- sunday

fun space

....
....
....

Today I AM open to the possibility of...

What I love about my work is...

Today I AM inspired to take these actions...

1.
2.
3.

I have a winning mindset and...

I AM
I AM
I AM
I AM

What have I learned today?

How was my mindset today?

What new habit do I want to adopt into my life?

How did I give value today?

date:

reminders

....
....
....
....
....
....

M & V meditation & visualisation
E exercise
I inspiration

6.00
7.00
8.00
9.00
10.00
11.00
12.00
13.00
14.00
15.00
16.00
17.00
18.00
19.00
20.00

genius space

....
....
....

Today, it would be fun to...

I AM so grateful for the simple things like...

What is the best course of action to take today?

1.
2.
3.

Today I AM creative and...

I AM
I AM
I AM
I AM

What was fantastic about today?

What skill can I develop further?

What new mindset do I want to adopt into my life?

What did I do really well today?

M & V meditation & visualisation
I inspiration
E exercise

- 6.00
- 7.00
- 8.00
- 9.00
- 10.00
- 11.00
- 12.00
- 13.00
- 14.00
- 15.00
- 16.00
- 17.00
- 18.00
- 19.00
- 20.00

date:

dream space

....
....
....

Today I would love....

I AM happy

Today I AM so grateful for...

My top 3 inspired actions for today are...

1.
2.
3.

My intentions for today are...

I AM
I AM
I AM
I AM

What was great about today?

What did I learn today?

After today, what behaviour do I want to upgrade?

What strengths did I use today?

date:

reminders

....
....
....
....
....
....
....

☐ **M & V** meditation & visualisation   ☐ **I** inspiration
☐ **E** exercise   ☐ ....

6.00
7.00
8.00
9.00
10.00
11.00
12.00
13.00
14.00
15.00
16.00
17.00
18.00
19.00
20.00

creative space

....
....
....

....
....
....
....
....
....
....
....

What if (insert possibility)....

Appreciation & Gratitude list...

M & V
meditation & visualisation

I
inspiration

E
exercise

Today, I AM most inspired to do these actions...

1.
2.
3.

....	6.00
....	7.00
....	8.00
....	9.00
....	10.00
....	11.00
....	12.00
....	13.00
....	14.00
....	15.00
....	16.00
....	17.00
....	18.00
....	19.00
....	20.00

The mindset I wish to create today is...

I AM
I AM
I AM
I AM

What did I enjoy about today?

What challenged me today that I can grow from?

What would I like to create instead?

What did I do really well today?

date:

ideas space

....
....
....

Today I accept that....

The things I AM grateful for in my life are...

Today, I would love to do these actions...

1.
2.
3.

Today I AM focusing on being...

I AM
I AM
I AM
I AM

What went well today?

What could I have handled differently today?

How can I open up to new ways of doing things?

What am I proud of about today?

date:

reminders

....
....
....
....
....
....
....

☐ **M & V** meditation & visualisation ☐ **I** inspiration
☐ **E** exercise ☐ ....

6.00
7.00
8.00
9.00
10.00
11.00
12.00
13.00
14.00
15.00
16.00
17.00
18.00
19.00
20.00

thoughts space

....
....
....

Today I AM going to create...

....
....
....
....
....
....
....

Gratitude is Wisdom...

M & V
meditation & visualisation

I
inspiration

E
exercise ....

Today, I feel inspired to do...

1.
2.
3.

_____	6.00
_____	7.00
_____	8.00
_____	9.00
_____	10.00
_____	11.00
_____	12.00
_____	13.00
_____	14.00
_____	15.00
_____	16.00
_____	17.00
_____	18.00
_____	19.00
_____	20.00

I create my day with my thoughts, therefore...

I AM
I AM
I AM
I AM

What did I love about today?

In what area would I like to grow?

What would I like to let go of?

How did I show leadership today?

date:

My week in review

Weekly Check-in

What projects have I completed this week?

☐ Review Greatness Blueprint

☐ Review Purpose Statement

What's going well and why is it?

☐ Update 90 Day Planner

☐ Add Actions To Weekly Planner

☐ Plan Your Week

What's most challenging and how can I turn it into an opportunity?

What is one thing I can do next week that will create the biggest results in my life?

8.00

9.00

10.00

11.00

What am I happy about right now?

12.00

13.00

14.00

How am I using my time? How can I prioritise better?

15.00

16.00

GET SOME ALTITUDE Where is my current attitude on a scale from 1-10? How can I get some more altitude and upgrade my attitude?

17.00

18.00

19.00

What fears are holding me back and how can I overcome those?

20.00

date:

Old Habit >	New Habit >	New Actions >	New Affirmation / Mantra

My goals for the next week

Weekly Planner

My mantra for this week is ....

4 Major Goals I'm Focused On This Week

| 1. | 2. | 3. | 4. |

| Projects & appointments for this week | Target date | Actions for this week | Target date |

monday

tuesday

wednesday

thursday

friday

saturday

sunday

open space

....

....

....

Today I AM going to enjoy...

When I AM grateful I open up to more...

What would I do today, if it was my last?

1.
2.
3.

Today...

I AM

I AM

I AM

I AM

What was interesting about today?

What habit would I like to develop after today?

What beliefs would I like to upgrade?

What strengths did I use today?

date:

reminders

....

....

....

....

....

....

....

....

☐ **M & V** meditation & visualisation   ☐ **I** inspiration
☐ **E** exercise   ☐ ....

6.00
7.00
8.00
9.00
10.00
11.00
12.00
13.00
14.00
15.00
16.00
17.00
18.00
19.00
20.00

invention space

....
....
....

Today is my opportunity to...

Today, I give thanks for...

My inspired actions for today are...

1.
2.
3.

Today I honor how I feel and...

I AM
I AM
I AM
I AM

What was fun about today?

What was today's lesson?

What new behaviour can I adopt into my life?

What did I succeed at...

M & V meditation & visualisation
I inspiration
E exercise

6.00
7.00
8.00
9.00
10.00
11.00
12.00
13.00
14.00
15.00
16.00
17.00
18.00
19.00
20.00

date:

fun space

....
....
....

Today I AM open to the possibility of...

What I love about my work is...

Today I AM inspired to take these actions...

1.
2.
3.

I have a winning mindset and...

I AM
I AM
I AM
I AM

What have I learned today?

How was my mindset today?

What new habit do I want to adopt into my life?

How did I give value today?

date:

reminders

....
....
....
....
....
....
....

☐ **M & V** meditation & visualisation   ☐ **I** inspiration
☐ **E** exercise   ☐ ....

6.00
7.00
8.00
9.00
10.00
11.00
12.00
13.00
14.00
15.00
16.00
17.00
18.00
19.00
20.00

genius space

....
....
....

Today, it would be fun to...

I AM so grateful for the simple things like...

M & V
meditation & visualisation

I
inspiration

E
exercise

....

What is the best course of action to take today?

1.
2.
3.

6.00	
7.00	
8.00	Today I AM creative and...
9.00	I AM
10.00	I AM
11.00	I AM
	I AM
12.00	What was fantastic about today?
13.00	
14.00	
15.00	What skill can I develop further?
16.00	
17.00	What new mindset do I want to adopt into my life?
18.00	
19.00	What did I do really well today?
20.00	

I AM open to receive

date:

dream space

....
....
....

Today I would love....

Today I AM so grateful for...

My top 3 inspired actions for today are...

1.
2.
3.

My intentions for today are...

I AM
I AM
I AM
I AM

What was great about today?

What did I learn today?

After today, what behaviour do I want to upgrade?

What strengths did I use today?

date:

reminders

....
....
....
....
....
....
....

☐ **M & V** meditation & visualisation   ☐ **I** inspiration
☐ **E** exercise   ☐ ....

6.00
7.00
8.00
9.00
10.00
11.00
12.00
13.00
14.00
15.00
16.00
17.00
18.00
19.00
20.00

… # creative space

………………………………………………………………

………………………………………………………………

………………………………………………………………

What if (insert possibility)….

Appreciation & Gratitude list…

M & V meditation & visualisation
I inspiration
E exercise
……………

Today, I AM most inspired to do these actions…

1.
2.
3.

The mindset I wish to create today is…

I AM
I AM
I AM
I AM

What did I enjoy about today?

What challenged me today that I can grow from?

What would I like to create instead?

What did I do really well today?

6.00
7.00
8.00
9.00
10.00
11.00
12.00
13.00
14.00
15.00
16.00
17.00
18.00
19.00
20.00

date:

My week in review

Weekly Check-in

What have I achieved on my greatness blueprint this week?

☐ Review Greatness Blueprint

☐ Review Purpose Statement

Where am I seeing the desired results & why?

☐ Update 90 Day Planner

☐ Add Actions To Weekly Planner

☐ Plan Your Week

What do I need to start or stop?

What is one thing I can do next week that will create the biggest results in my life?

Where can I be a better leader?

Do I need to upgrade my communication skills? How can I be better?

GET SOME ALTITUDE Where is my current attitude on a scale from 1-10? How can I get some more altitude and upgrade my attitude?

What negative attitudes are holding me back and how can I overcome those?

8.00
9.00
10.00
11.00
12.00
13.00
14.00
15.00
16.00
17.00
18.00
19.00
20.00

date:

Old Habit >   New Habit >   New Actions >   New Affirmation / Mantra

My goals for the next week

Weekly Planner

My mantra for this week is ....

4 Major Goals I'm Focused On This Week

1.　　　　　　　2.　　　　　　　3.　　　　　　　4.

| Projects & appointments for this week | Target date | Actions for this week | Target date |

monday

tuesday

wednesday

thursday

friday

saturday

sunday

ideas space

....
....
....

Today I accept that....

The things I AM grateful for in my life are...

Today, I would love to do these actions...
1.
2.
3.

Today I AM focusing on being...

I AM
I AM
I AM
I AM

What went well today?

What could I have handled differently today?

How can I open up to new ways of doing things?

What am I proud of about today?

date:

reminders

....
....
....
....
....
....

☐ **M & V** meditation & visualisation   ☐ **I** inspiration
☐ **E** exercise   ☐ ....

6.00
7.00
8.00
9.00
10.00
11.00
12.00
13.00
14.00
15.00
16.00
17.00
18.00
19.00
20.00

thoughts space

....
....
....

Today I AM going to create...

Gratitude is Wisdom...

M & V meditation & visualisation
I inspiration
E exercise

Today, I feel inspired to do...

1.
2.
3.

I create my day with my thoughts, therefore...

I AM
I AM
I AM
I AM

What did I love about today?

In what area would I like to grow?

What would I like to let go of?

How did I show leadership today?

6.00
7.00
8.00
9.00
10.00
11.00
12.00
13.00
14.00
15.00
16.00
17.00
18.00
19.00
20.00

date:

open space

....
....
....

Today I AM going to enjoy...

When I AM grateful I open up to more...

What would I do today, if it was my last?
1.
2.
3.

Today...
I AM
I AM
I AM
I AM

What was interesting about today?

What habit would I like to develop after today?

What beliefs would I like to upgrade?

What strengths did I use today?

date:

I AM open to receive

reminders

....
....
....
....
....
....
....

☐ **M & V** meditation & visualisation ☐ **I** inspiration
☐ **E** exercise ☐ ....

6.00
7.00
8.00
9.00
10.00
11.00
12.00
13.00
14.00
15.00
16.00
17.00
18.00
19.00
20.00

invention space

....

....

....

Today is my opportunity to...

Today, I give thanks for...

M & V meditation & visualisation

I inspiration

E exercise

My inspired actions for today are...

1.
2.
3.

6.00	Today I honor how I feel and...
7.00	I AM
8.00	I AM
9.00	I AM
10.00	I AM
11.00	
12.00	What was fun about today?
13.00	
14.00	What was today's lesson?
15.00	
16.00	
17.00	What new behaviour can I adopt into my life?
18.00	
19.00	What did I succeed at...
20.00	

date:

fun space

....
....
....

Today I AM open to the possibility of...

What I love about my work is...

Today I AM inspired to take these actions...

1.
2.
3.

I have a winning mindset and...

I AM
I AM
I AM
I AM

What have I learned today?

How was my mindset today?

What new habit do I want to adopt into my life?

How did I give value today?

date:

reminders

....
....
....
....
....
....
....
....

☐ **M & V** meditation & visualisation   ☐ **I** inspiration
☐ **E** exercise   ☐ ....

6.00
7.00
8.00
9.00
10.00
11.00
12.00
13.00
14.00
15.00
16.00
17.00
18.00
19.00
20.00

genius space

....
....
....

Today, it would be fun to...

I AM so grateful for the simple things like...

M & V meditation & visualisation
I inspiration
E exercise
....

What is the best course of action to take today?

1.
2.
3.

Today I AM creative and...

I AM
I AM
I AM
I AM

What was fantastic about today?

What skill can I develop further?

What new mindset do I want to adopt into my life?

What did I do really well today?

- 6.00
- 7.00
- 8.00
- 9.00
- 10.00
- 11.00
- 12.00
- 13.00
- 14.00
- 15.00
- 16.00
- 17.00
- 18.00
- 19.00
- 20.00

date:

My week in review

Weekly Check-in

What major goals have I achieved this month?

☐ Review Greatness Blueprint

☐ Review Purpose Statement

Where am I having success and why?

☐ Update 90 Day Planner

☐ Add Actions To Weekly Planner

☐ Plan Your Week

What are the biggest distractions in my life and how can I remove them?

What is one thing I can do next week that will create the biggest results in my life?

What am I committed to achieving in my life right now?

What is my home and work environment like? Does it inspire me?

GET SOME ALTITUDE Where is my current attitude on a scale from 1-10? How can I get some more altitude and upgrade my attitude?

What disempowering thoughts are holding me back and how can I upgrade those?

date:

8.00
9.00
10.00
11.00
12.00
13.00
14.00
15.00
16.00
17.00
18.00
19.00
20.00

Old Habit >	New Habit >	New Actions >	New Affirmation / Mantra

My goals for the next week

Weekly Planner

My mantra for this week is ....

4 Major Goals I'm Focused On This Week

| 1. | 2. | 3. | 4. |

Projects & appointments for this week	Target date	Actions for this week	Target date

monday

tuesday

wednesday

thursday

friday

saturday

sunday

dream space

....
....
....

Today I would love....

Today I AM so grateful for...

My top 3 inspired actions for today are...

1.
2.
3.

My intentions for today are...

I AM
I AM
I AM
I AM

What was great about today?

What did I learn today?

After today, what behaviour do I want to upgrade?

What strengths did I use today?

date:

reminders

....
....
....
....
....
....
....

☐ **M & V** meditation & visualisation   ☐ **I** inspiration
☐ **E** exercise   ☐ ....

6.00
....
7.00
....
8.00
....
9.00
....
10.00
....
11.00
....
12.00
....
13.00
....
14.00
....
15.00
....
16.00
....
17.00
....
18.00
....
19.00
....
20.00
....

creative space

....
....
....

What if (insert possibility)....

Appreciation & Gratitude list...

M & V meditation & visualisation
I inspiration
E exercise

Today, I AM most inspired to do these actions...

1.
2.
3.

The mindset I wish to create today is...

I AM
I AM
I AM
I AM

Time
6.00
7.00
8.00
9.00
10.00
11.00
12.00
13.00
14.00
15.00
16.00
17.00
18.00
19.00
20.00

What did I enjoy about today?

What challenged me today that I can grow from?

What would I like to create instead?

What did I do really well today?

date:

ideas space

....
....
....

Today I accept that....

The things I AM grateful for in my life are...

Today, I would love to do these actions...

1.
2.
3.

Today I AM focusing on being...

I AM
I AM
I AM
I AM

What went well today?

What could I have handled differently today?

How can I open up to new ways of doing things?

What am I proud of about today?

date:

reminders

....
....
....
....
....
....
....
....

☐ **M & V** meditation & visualisation   ☐ **I** inspiration
☐ **E** exercise   ☐ ....

6.00
7.00
8.00
9.00
10.00
11.00
12.00
13.00
14.00
15.00
16.00
17.00
18.00
19.00
20.00

thoughts space

....
....
....

Today I AM going to create...

Gratitude is Wisdom...

M & V
meditation & visualisation

I
inspiration

E
exercise

Today, I feel inspired to do...

1.
2.
3.

6.00
7.00
8.00
9.00
10.00
11.00
12.00
13.00
14.00
15.00
16.00
17.00
18.00
19.00
20.00

I create my day with my thoughts, therefore...

I AM
I AM
I AM
I AM

What did I love about today?

In what area would I like to grow?

What would I like to let go of?

How did I show leadership today?

date:

open space

....
....
....

Today I AM going to enjoy...

When I AM grateful I open up to more...

What would I do today, if it was my last?

1.
2.
3.

Today...
I AM
I AM
I AM
I AM

What was interesting about today?

What habit would I like to develop after today?

What beliefs would I like to upgrade?

What strengths did I use today?

date:

reminders

....
....
....
....
....
....

☐ **M & V** meditation & visualisation   ☐ **I** inspiration
☐ **E** exercise   ☐ ....

6.00
7.00
8.00
9.00
10.00
11.00
12.00
13.00
14.00
15.00
16.00
17.00
18.00
19.00
20.00

invention space

....
....
....

Today is my opportunity to...

Today, I give thanks for...

M & V meditation & visualisation
I inspiration
E exercise

My inspired actions for today are...

1.
2.
3.

6.00
7.00
8.00
9.00
10.00
11.00
12.00
13.00
14.00
15.00
16.00
17.00
18.00
19.00
20.00

Today I honor how I feel and...

I AM
I AM
I AM
I AM

What was fun about today?

What was today's lesson?

What new behaviour can I adopt into my life?

What did I succeed at...

date:

My week in review

Weekly Check-in

What have I achieved this week?

☐ Review Greatness Blueprint

☐ Review Purpose Statement

What's working and why is it working?

☐ Update 90 Day Planner

☐ Add Actions To Weekly Planner

☐ Plan Your Week

What's not working and what am I willing to do about it?

8.00

9.00

What is one thing I can do next week that will create the biggest results in my life?

10.00

11.00

What do I need to make a decision about?

12.00

13.00

14.00

Have I had fun this week? How can I have more fun?

15.00

date:

16.00

GET SOME ALTITUDE Where is my current attitude on a scale from 1-10? How can I get some more altitude and upgrade my attitude?

17.00

18.00

19.00

What beliefs are holding me back and how can I upgrade those?

20.00

| Old Habit > | New Habit > | New Actions > | New Affirmation / Mantra |

My goals for the next week

Weekly Planner

My mantra for this week is ....

4 Major Goals I'm Focused On This Week

1.　　　　　　　2.　　　　　　　3.　　　　　　　4.

Projects & appointments for this week	Target date	Actions for this week	Target date

- monday
- tuesday
- wednesday
- thursday
- friday
- saturday
- sunday

fun space

....
....
....

Today I AM open to the possibility of...

What I love about my work is...

Today I AM inspired to take these actions...

1.
2.
3.

I have a winning mindset and...

I AM
I AM
I AM
I AM

What have I learned today?

How was my mindset today?

What new habit do I want to adopt into my life?

How did I give value today?

date:

reminders

....
....
....
....
....
....

☐ **M & V** meditation & visualisation ☐ **I** inspiration
☐ **E** exercise ☐ ....

6.00
....
7.00
....
8.00
....
9.00
....
10.00
....
11.00
....
12.00
....
13.00
....
14.00
....
15.00
....
16.00
....
17.00
....
18.00
....
19.00
....
20.00
....

genius space

....
....
....

Today, it would be fun to...

I AM so grateful for the simple things like...

M & V
meditation & visualisation

I
inspiration

E
exercise

What is the best course of action to take today?

1.
2.
3.

Today I AM creative and...

I AM
I AM
I AM
I AM

What was fantastic about today?

6.00
7.00
8.00
9.00
10.00
11.00
12.00
13.00
14.00

What skill can I develop further?

15.00
16.00
17.00

What new mindset do I want to adopt into my life?

18.00
19.00

What did I do really well today?

20.00

I AM open to receive

date:

dream space

....
....
....

Today I would love....

Today I AM so grateful for...

My top 3 inspired actions for today are...

1.
2.
3.

My intentions for today are...

I AM
I AM
I AM
I AM

What was great about today?

What did I learn today?

After today, what behaviour do I want to upgrade?

What strengths did I use today?

date:

reminders

....
....
....
....
....
....
....

☐ **M & V** meditation & visualisation   ☐ **I** inspiration
☐ **E** exercise   ☐ ....

6.00
7.00
8.00
9.00
10.00
11.00
12.00
13.00
14.00
15.00
16.00
17.00
18.00
19.00
20.00

creative space

....
....
....

What if (insert possibility)....

Appreciation & Gratitude list...

Today, I AM most inspired to do these actions...

1.
2.
3.

The mindset I wish to create today is...

I AM
I AM
I AM
I AM

What did I enjoy about today?

What challenged me today that I can grow from?

What would I like to create instead?

What did I do really well today?

M & V meditation & visualisation
I inspiration
E exercise

6.00
7.00
8.00
9.00
10.00
11.00
12.00
13.00
14.00
15.00
16.00
17.00
18.00
19.00
20.00

date:

ideas space

....

....

....

Today I accept that....

The things I AM grateful for in my life are...

Today, I would love to do these actions...

1.
2.
3.

Today I AM focusing on being...

I AM

I AM

I AM

I AM

What went well today?

What could I have handled differently today?

How can I open up to new ways of doing things?

What am I proud of about today?

date:

reminders

....

....

....

....

....

....

....

□ **M & V** meditation & visualisation   □ **I** inspiration

□ **E** exercise   □ ....

6.00
7.00
8.00
9.00
10.00
11.00
12.00
13.00
14.00
15.00
16.00
17.00
18.00
19.00
20.00

thoughts space

....
....
....

Today I AM going to create...

Gratitude is Wisdom...

M & V
meditation & visualisation

I
inspiration

E
exercise

Today, I feel inspired to do...

1.
2.
3.

6.00
7.00
8.00
9.00
10.00
11.00
12.00
13.00
14.00
15.00
16.00
17.00
18.00
19.00
20.00

I create my day with my thoughts, therefore...

I AM
I AM
I AM
I AM

What did I love about today?

In what area would I like to grow?

What would I like to let go of?

How did I show leadership today?

date:

My week in review

Weekly Check-in

What projects have I completed this week?

☐ Review Greatness Blueprint

☐ Review Purpose Statement

☐ Update 90 Day Planner

What's going well and why is it?

☐ Add Actions To Weekly Planner

☐ Plan Your Week

What's most challenging and how can I turn it into an opportunity?

8.00

9.00

What is one thing I can do next week that will create the biggest results in my life?

10.00

11.00

12.00

What am I happy about right now?

13.00

14.00

date:

How am I using my time? How can I prioritise better?

15.00

16.00

GET SOME ALTITUDE Where is my current attitude on a scale from 1-10? How can I get some more altitude and upgrade my attitude?

17.00

18.00

19.00

What fears are holding me back and how can I overcome those?

20.00

Old Habit >	New Habit >	New Actions >	New Affirmation / Mantra

My goals for the next week

Weekly Planner

My mantra for this week is ....

4 Major Goals I'm Focused On This Week

1.
2.
3.
4.

Projects & appointments for this week	Target date	Actions for this week	Target date

monday

tuesday

wednesday

thursday

friday

saturday

sunday

open space

....
....
....

Today I AM going to enjoy...

When I AM grateful I open up to more...

What would I do today, if it was my last?
1.
2.
3.

Today...
I AM
I AM
I AM
I AM

What was interesting about today?

What habit would I like to develop after today?

What beliefs would I like to upgrade?

What strengths did I use today?

date:

reminders

....
....
....
....
....
....
....

☐ **M & V** meditation & visualisation ☐ **I** inspiration
☐ **E** exercise ☐ ....

6.00
7.00
8.00
9.00
10.00
11.00
12.00
13.00
14.00
15.00
16.00
17.00
18.00
19.00
20.00

invention space

....
....
....

Today is my opportunity to...

Today, I give thanks for...

M & V meditation & visualisation
I inspiration
E exercise

My inspired actions for today are...

1.
2.
3.

	6.00
	7.00
	8.00
	9.00
	10.00
	11.00
	12.00
	13.00
	14.00
	15.00
	16.00
	17.00
	18.00
	19.00
	20.00

Today I honor how I feel and...

I AM
I AM
I AM
I AM

What was fun about today?

What was today's lesson?

What new behaviour can I adopt into my life?

What did I succeed at...

date:

fun space

....
....
....

Today I AM open to the possibility of...

What I love about my work is...

Today I AM inspired to take these actions...

1.
2.
3.

I have a winning mindset and...

I AM
I AM
I AM
I AM

What have I learned today?

How was my mindset today?

What new habit do I want to adopt into my life?

How did I give value today?

date:

reminders

....
....
....
....
....
....

☐ **M & V** meditation & visualisation   ☐ **I** inspiration
☐ **E** exercise   ☐ ....

6.00
7.00
8.00
9.00
10.00
11.00
12.00
13.00
14.00
15.00
16.00
17.00
18.00
19.00
20.00

genius space

....
....
....

....
....
....
....

Today, it would be fun to...

I AM so grateful for the simple things like...

M & V meditation & visualisation
I inspiration
E exercise

What is the best course of action to take today?
1.
2.
3.

6.00
7.00
8.00

Today I AM creative and...

I AM
I AM
I AM
I AM

9.00
10.00
11.00
12.00

What was fantastic about today?

13.00
14.00

What skill can I develop further?

15.00
16.00
17.00

What new mindset do I want to adopt into my life?

18.00
19.00

What did I do really well today?

20.00

I AM happy

date:

dream space

....
....
....

Today I would love....

Today I AM so grateful for...

My top 3 inspired actions for today are...

1.
2.
3.

My intentions for today are...

I AM
I AM
I AM
I AM

What was great about today?

What did I learn today?

After today, what behaviour do I want to upgrade?

What strengths did I use today?

date:

reminders

....
....
....
....
....
....
....

☐ **M & V** meditation & visualisation   ☐ **I** inspiration
☐ **E** exercise   ☐ ....

6.00
7.00
8.00
9.00
10.00
11.00
12.00
13.00
14.00
15.00
16.00
17.00
18.00
19.00
20.00

creative space

....
....
....

What if (insert possibility)....

Appreciation & Gratitude list...

Today, I AM most inspired to do these actions...

1.
2.
3.

The mindset I wish to create today is...

I AM
I AM
I AM
I AM

What did I enjoy about today?

What challenged me today that I can grow from?

What would I like to create instead?

What did I do really well today?

M & V meditation & visualisation
I inspiration
E exercise

6.00
7.00
8.00
9.00
10.00
11.00
12.00
13.00
14.00
15.00
16.00
17.00
18.00
19.00
20.00

date:

My week in review

Weekly Check-in

What have I achieved on my greatness blueprint this week?

☐ Review Greatness Blueprint

☐ Review Purpose Statement

☐ Update 90 Day Planner

Where am I seeing the desired results & why?

☐ Add Actions To Weekly Planner

☐ Plan Your Week

What do I need to start or stop?

8.00

9.00

What is one thing I can do next week that will create the biggest results in my life?

10.00

11.00

12.00

Where can I be a better leader?

13.00

14.00

date:

Do I need to upgrade my communication skills? How can I be better?

15.00

16.00

GET SOME ALTITUDE Where is my current attitude on a scale from 1-10? How can I get some more altitude and upgrade my attitude?

17.00

18.00

19.00

What negative attitudes are holding me back and how can I overcome those?

20.00

| Old Habit > | New Habit > | New Actions > | New Affirmation / Mantra |

My goals for the next week

Weekly Planner

My mantra for this week is
....

4 Major Goals I'm Focused On This Week

1.
2.
3.
4.

Projects & appointments for this week	Target date	Actions for this week	Target date

monday

tuesday

wednesday

thursday

friday

saturday

sunday

ideas space

....
....
....

Today I accept that....

The things I AM grateful for in my life are...

Today, I would love to do these actions...

1.
2.
3.

Today I AM focusing on being...

I AM
I AM
I AM
I AM

What went well today?

What could I have handled differently today?

How can I open up to new ways of doing things?

What am I proud of about today?

date:

reminders

....
....
....
....
....
....
....

☐ **M & V** meditation & visualisation   ☐ **I** inspiration
☐ **E** exercise   ☐ ....

6.00
7.00
8.00
9.00
10.00
11.00
12.00
13.00
14.00
15.00
16.00
17.00
18.00
19.00
20.00

thoughts space

....
....
....

Today I AM going to create...

Gratitude is Wisdom...

M & V meditation & visualisation
I inspiration
E exercise

Today, I feel inspired to do...
1.
2.
3.

I create my day with my thoughts, therefore...
I AM
I AM
I AM
I AM

What did I love about today?

In what area would I like to grow?

What would I like to let go of?

How did I show leadership today?

6.00
7.00
8.00
9.00
10.00
11.00
12.00
13.00
14.00
15.00
16.00
17.00
18.00
19.00
20.00

date:

open space

....
....
....

Today I AM going to enjoy...

When I AM grateful I open up to more...

What would I do today, if it was my last?
1.
2.
3.

Today...
I AM
I AM
I AM
I AM

What was interesting about today?

What habit would I like to develop after today?

What beliefs would I like to upgrade?

What strengths did I use today?

date:

reminders

....
....
....
....
....
....
....

☐ **M & V** meditation & visualisation   ☐ **I** inspiration
☐ **E** exercise   ☐ ....

6.00
7.00
8.00
9.00
10.00
11.00
12.00
13.00
14.00
15.00
16.00
17.00
18.00
19.00
20.00

I AM open to receive

invention space

....
....
....

Today is my opportunity to...

Today, I give thanks for...

My inspired actions for today are...

1.
2.
3.

Today I honor how I feel and...

I AM
I AM
I AM
I AM

What was fun about today?

What was today's lesson?

What new behaviour can I adopt into my life?

What did I succeed at...

M & V
meditation & visualisation

I
inspiration

E
exercise

6.00
7.00
8.00
9.00
10.00
11.00
12.00
13.00
14.00
15.00
16.00
17.00
18.00
19.00
20.00

date:

fun space

....
....
....

Today I AM open to the possibility of...

What I love about my work is...

Today I AM inspired to take these actions...

1.
2.
3.

I have a winning mindset and...

I AM
I AM
I AM
I AM

What have I learned today?

How was my mindset today?

What new habit do I want to adopt into my life?

How did I give value today?

date:

reminders

....
....
....
....
....
....
....
....

☐ **M & V** meditation & visualisation   ☐ **I** inspiration
☐ **E** exercise   ☐ ....

6.00
7.00
8.00
9.00
10.00
11.00
12.00
13.00
14.00
15.00
16.00
17.00
18.00
19.00
20.00

genius space

....
....
....

Today, it would be fun to...

I AM so grateful for the simple things like...

M & V meditation & visualisation
I inspiration
E exercise
....

What is the best course of action to take today?

1.
2.
3.

Today I AM creative and...

I AM
I AM
I AM
I AM

What was fantastic about today?

What skill can I develop further?

What new mindset do I want to adopt into my life?

What did I do really well today?

6.00
7.00
8.00
9.00
10.00
11.00
12.00
13.00
14.00
15.00
16.00
17.00
18.00
19.00
20.00

date:

My week in review

Weekly Check-in

What major goals have I achieved this month?

- [ ] Review Greatness Blueprint
- [ ] Review Purpose Statement
- [ ] Update 90 Day Planner
- [ ] Add Actions To Weekly Planner
- [ ] Plan Your Week

Where am I having success and why?

What are the biggest distractions in my life and how can I remove them?

What is one thing I can do next week that will create the biggest results in my life?

What am I committed to achieving in my life right now?

date:

What is my home and work environment like? Does it inspire me?

GET SOME ALTITUDE Where is my current attitude on a scale from 1-10? How can I get some more altitude and upgrade my attitude?

What disempowering thoughts are holding me back and how can I upgrade those?

8.00
9.00
10.00
11.00
12.00
13.00
14.00
15.00
16.00
17.00
18.00
19.00
20.00

Old Habit >	New Habit >	New Actions >	New Affirmation / Mantra

My goals for the next week

Weekly Planner

My mantra for this week is ....

4 Major Goals I'm Focused On This Week

| 1. | 2. | 3. | 4. |

| Projects & appointments for this week | Target date | Actions for this week | Target date |

- monday
- tuesday
- wednesday
- thursday
- friday
- saturday
- sunday

dream space

....
....
....

Today I would love....

Today I AM so grateful for...

My top 3 inspired actions for today are...

1.
2.
3.

My intentions for today are...

I AM
I AM
I AM
I AM

What was great about today?

What did I learn today?

After today, what behaviour do I want to upgrade?

What strengths did I use today?

date:

reminders

....
....
....
....
....
....
....

☐ **M & V** meditation & visualisation   ☐ **I** inspiration
☐ **E** exercise   ☐ ....

6.00
....
7.00
....
8.00
....
9.00
....
10.00
....
11.00
....
12.00
....
13.00
....
14.00
....
15.00
....
16.00
....
17.00
....
18.00
....
19.00
....
20.00

creative space

....
....
....

....
....

What if (insert possibility)....

Appreciation & Gratitude list...

M & V
meditation & visualisation

I
inspiration

E
exercise

....

Today, I AM most inspired to do these actions...

1.
2.
3.

	6.00
	7.00
	8.00
	9.00
	10.00
	11.00
	12.00
	13.00
	14.00
	15.00
	16.00
	17.00
	18.00
	19.00
	20.00

The mindset I wish to create today is...

I AM
I AM
I AM
I AM

What did I enjoy about today?

What challenged me today that I can grow from?

What would I like to create instead?

What did I do really well today?

date:

date:

ideas space

....
....
....

Today I accept that....

The things I AM grateful for in my life are...

Today, I would love to do these actions...

1.
2.
3.

Today I AM focusing on being...

I AM
I AM
I AM
I AM

What went well today?

What could I have handled differently today?

How can I open up to new ways of doing things?

What am I proud of about today?

reminders

....
....
....
....
....
....
....

☐ **M & V** meditation & visualisation   ☐ **I** inspiration
☐ **E** exercise   ☐ ....

6.00
7.00
8.00
9.00
10.00
11.00
12.00
13.00
14.00
15.00
16.00
17.00
18.00
19.00
20.00

thoughts space

....
....
....

Today I AM going to create...

Gratitude is Wisdom...

M & V meditation & visualisation
I inspiration
E exercise

Today, I feel inspired to do...

1.
2.
3.

I create my day with my thoughts, therefore...

I AM
I AM
I AM
I AM

What did I love about today?

In what area would I like to grow?

What would I like to let go of?

How did I show leadership today?

6.00
7.00
8.00
9.00
10.00
11.00
12.00
13.00
14.00
15.00
16.00
17.00
18.00
19.00
20.00

date:

open space

....
....
....

Today I AM going to enjoy...

When I AM grateful I open up to more...

What would I do today, if it was my last?
1.
2.
3.

Today...
I AM
I AM
I AM
I AM

What was interesting about today?

What habit would I like to develop after today?

What beliefs would I like to upgrade?

What strengths did I use today?

date:

I AM happy

reminders

....
....
....
....
....
....
....

☐ **M & V** meditation & visualisation ☐ **I** inspiration
☐ **E** exercise ☐ ....

6.00 ....
7.00 ....
8.00 ....
9.00 ....
10.00 ....
11.00 ....
12.00 ....
13.00 ....
14.00 ....
15.00 ....
16.00 ....
17.00 ....
18.00 ....
19.00 ....
20.00 ....

invention space

....
....
....

Today is my opportunity to...

Today, I give thanks for...

My inspired actions for today are...

1.
2.
3.

Today I honor how I feel and...

I AM
I AM
I AM
I AM

What was fun about today?

What was today's lesson?

What new behaviour can I adopt into my life?

What did I succeed at...

M & V meditation & visualisation
I inspiration
E exercise

6.00
7.00
8.00
9.00
10.00
11.00
12.00
13.00
14.00
15.00
16.00
17.00
18.00
19.00
20.00

date:

My week in review

Weekly Check-in

What have I achieved this week?

- [ ] Review Greatness Blueprint
- [ ] Review Purpose Statement
- [ ] Update 90 Day Planner
- [ ] Add Actions To Weekly Planner
- [ ] Plan Your Week

What's working and why is it working?

What's not working and what am I willing to do about it?

What is one thing I can do next week that will create the biggest results in my life?

What do I need to make a decision about?

Have I had fun this week? How can I have more fun?

GET SOME ALTITUDE Where is my current attitude on a scale from 1-10? How can I get some more altitude and upgrade my attitude?

What beliefs are holding me back and how can I upgrade those?

8.00
9.00
10.00
11.00
12.00
13.00
14.00
15.00
16.00
17.00
18.00
19.00
20.00

date:

Old Habit >	New Habit >	New Actions >	New Affirmation / Mantra

My goals for the next week

Weekly Planner

My mantra for this week is ....

4 Major Goals I'm Focused On This Week

| 1. | 2. | 3. | 4. |

| Projects & appointments for this week | Target date | Actions for this week | Target date |

monday

tuesday

wednesday

thursday

friday

saturday

sunday

fun space

....
....
....

Today I AM open to the possibility of...

What I love about my work is...

Today I AM inspired to take these actions...
1.
2.
3.

I have a winning mindset and...
I AM
I AM
I AM
I AM

What have I learned today?

How was my mindset today?

What new habit do I want to adopt into my life?

How did I give value today?

date:

reminders

....
....
....
....
....
....
....

☐ **M & V** meditation & visualisation   ☐ **I** inspiration
☐ **E** exercise   ☐ ....

6.00
7.00
8.00
9.00
10.00
11.00
12.00
13.00
14.00
15.00
16.00
17.00
18.00
19.00
20.00

… … … … … … … … …

… … … … … … … … …

… … … … … … … … …

genius space

……………………………………………………………………………………

……………………………………………………………………………………

……………………………………………………………………………………

Today, it would be fun to...

I AM so grateful for the simple things like...

M & V meditation & visualisation
I inspiration
E exercise

What is the best course of action to take today?

1.
2.
3.

Today I AM creative and...

I AM
I AM
I AM
I AM

_____	6.00
_____	7.00
_____	8.00
_____	9.00
_____	10.00
_____	11.00
_____	12.00
_____	13.00
_____	14.00
_____	15.00
_____	16.00
_____	17.00
_____	18.00
_____	19.00
_____	20.00

What was fantastic about today?

What skill can I develop further?

What new mindset do I want to adopt into my life?

What did I do really well today?

date:

dream space

....
....
....

Today I would love....

I AM open to receive

Today I AM so grateful for...

My top 3 inspired actions for today are...

1.
2.
3.

My intentions for today are...

I AM
I AM
I AM
I AM

What was great about today?

What did I learn today?

After today, what behaviour do I want to upgrade?

What strengths did I use today?

date:

reminders

....
....
....
....
....
....
....
....

☐ **M & V** meditation & visualisation   ☐ **I** inspiration
☐ **E** exercise   ☐ ....

6.00
7.00
8.00
9.00
10.00
11.00
12.00
13.00
14.00
15.00
16.00
17.00
18.00
19.00
20.00

creative space

....
....
....

What if (insert possibility)....

Appreciation & Gratitude list...

Today, I AM most inspired to do these actions...

1.
2.
3.

The mindset I wish to create today is...

I AM
I AM
I AM
I AM

What did I enjoy about today?

What challenged me today that I can grow from?

What would I like to create instead?

What did I do really well today?

M & V meditation & visualisation
I inspiration
E exercise

6.00
7.00
8.00
9.00
10.00
11.00
12.00
13.00
14.00
15.00
16.00
17.00
18.00
19.00
20.00

date:

ideas space

....
....
....

Today I accept that....

The things I AM grateful for in my life are...

Today, I would love to do these actions...

1.
2.
3.

Today I AM focusing on being...

I AM
I AM
I AM
I AM

What went well today?

What could I have handled differently today?

How can I open up to new ways of doing things?

What am I proud of about today?

date:

reminders

....
....
....
....
....
....
....

☐ **M & V** meditation & visualisation ☐ **I** inspiration
☐ **E** exercise ☐ ....

6.00
7.00
8.00
9.00
10.00
11.00
12.00
13.00
14.00
15.00
16.00
17.00
18.00
19.00
20.00

thoughts space

....

....

....

Today I AM going to create…

Gratitude is Wisdom…

Today, I feel inspired to do…

1.
2.
3.

I create my day with my thoughts, therefore…

I AM

I AM

I AM

I AM

What did I love about today?

In what area would I like to grow?

What would I like to let go of?

How did I show leadership today?

M & V meditation & visualisation
I inspiration
E exercise

- 6.00
- 7.00
- 8.00
- 9.00
- 10.00
- 11.00
- 12.00
- 13.00
- 14.00
- 15.00
- 16.00
- 17.00
- 18.00
- 19.00
- 20.00

date:

My week in review

Weekly Check-in

What projects have I completed this week?

- [ ] Review Greatness Blueprint
- [ ] Review Purpose Statement
- [ ] Update 90 Day Planner
- [ ] Add Actions To Weekly Planner
- [ ] Plan Your Week

What's going well and why is it?

What's most challenging and how can I turn it into an opportunity?

What is one thing I can do next week that will create the biggest results in my life?

What am I happy about right now?

How am I using my time? How can I prioritise better?

GET SOME ALTITUDE Where is my current attitude on a scale from 1-10? How can I get some more altitude and upgrade my attitude?

What fears are holding me back and how can I overcome those?

date:

8.00
9.00
10.00
11.00
12.00
13.00
14.00
15.00
16.00
17.00
18.00
19.00
20.00

| Old Habit > | New Habit > | New Actions > | New Affirmation / Mantra |

My goals for the next week

Weekly Planner

My mantra for this week is ....

4 Major Goals I'm Focused On This Week

1.	2.	3.	4.

Projects & appointments for this week	Target date	Actions for this week	Target date
monday			
tuesday			
wednesday			
thursday			
friday			
saturday			
sunday			

open space

....
....
....

Today I AM going to enjoy...

When I AM grateful I open up to more...

What would I do today, if it was my last?
1.
2.
3.

Today...
I AM
I AM
I AM
I AM

What was interesting about today?

What habit would I like to develop after today?

What beliefs would I like to upgrade?

What strengths did I use today?

date:

reminders

....
....
....
....
....
....
....

☐ **M & V** meditation & visualisation   ☐ **I** inspiration
☐ **E** exercise   ☐ ....

6.00
7.00
8.00
9.00
10.00
11.00
12.00
13.00
14.00
15.00
16.00
17.00
18.00
19.00
20.00

invention space

....
....
....
....
.... Today is my opportunity to...
....
....
.... Today, I give thanks for...
....

M & V meditation & visualisation   **I** inspiration
E exercise   ☐ ....

My inspired actions for today are...

1.
2.
3.

Today I honor how I feel and...

I AM
I AM
I AM
I AM

What was fun about today?

What was today's lesson?

What new behaviour can I adopt into my life?

What did I succeed at...

Time	
6.00	
7.00	
8.00	
9.00	
10.00	
11.00	
12.00	
13.00	
14.00	
15.00	
16.00	
17.00	
18.00	
19.00	
20.00	

date:

fun space

....
....
....

Today I AM open to the possibility of...

What I love about my work is...

Today I AM inspired to take these actions...

1.
2.
3.

I have a winning mindset and...

I AM
I AM
I AM
I AM

What have I learned today?

How was my mindset today?

What new habit do I want to adopt into my life?

How did I give value today?

date:

reminders

....
....
....
....
....
....
....

☐ **M & V** meditation & visualisation   ☐ **I** inspiration
☐ **E** exercise   ☐ ....

6.00
7.00
8.00
9.00
10.00
11.00
12.00
13.00
14.00
15.00
16.00
17.00
18.00
19.00
20.00

genius space

....
....
....

Today, it would be fun to...

I AM so grateful for the simple things like...

What is the best course of action to take today?

1.
2.
3.

Today I AM creative and...

I AM
I AM
I AM
I AM

What was fantastic about today?

What skill can I develop further?

What new mindset do I want to adopt into my life?

What did I do really well today?

....
....
....
....
....
....
....
....

M & V meditation & visualisation
I inspiration
E exercise

6.00
7.00
8.00
9.00
10.00
11.00
12.00
13.00
14.00
15.00
16.00
17.00
18.00
19.00
20.00

date:

I AM happy

dream space

....
....
....

Today I would love....

Today I AM so grateful for...

My top 3 inspired actions for today are...

1.
2.
3.

My intentions for today are...

I AM
I AM
I AM
I AM

date:

What was great about today?

What did I learn today?

After today, what behaviour do I want to upgrade?

What strengths did I use today?

reminders

....
....
....
....
....
....
....
....

☐ **M & V** meditation & visualisation   ☐ **I** inspiration
☐ **E** exercise   ☐ ....

6.00
7.00
8.00
9.00
10.00
11.00
12.00
13.00
14.00
15.00
16.00
17.00
18.00
19.00
20.00

creative space

....
....
....

What if (insert possibility)....

Appreciation & Gratitude list...

M & V meditation & visualisation
I inspiration
E exercise

Today, I AM most inspired to do these actions...

1.
2.
3.

The mindset I wish to create today is...

I AM
I AM
I AM
I AM

What did I enjoy about today?

6.00
7.00
8.00
9.00
10.00
11.00
12.00
13.00
14.00
15.00
16.00
17.00
18.00
19.00
20.00

What challenged me today that I can grow from?

What would I like to create instead?

What did I do really well today?

date:

My week in review

Weekly Check-in

What have I achieved on my greatness blueprint this week?

- [ ] Review Greatness Blueprint
- [ ] Review Purpose Statement
- [ ] Update 90 Day Planner
- [ ] Add Actions To Weekly Planner
- [ ] Plan Your Week

Where am I seeing the desired results & why?

What do I need to start or stop?

What is one thing I can do next week that will create the biggest results in my life?

Where can I be a better leader?

Do I need to upgrade my communication skills? How can I be better?

GET SOME ALTITUDE Where is my current attitude on a scale from 1 -10? How can I get some more altitude and upgrade my attitude?

What negative attitudes are holding me back and how can I overcome those?

date:

8.00
9.00
10.00
11.00
12.00
13.00
14.00
15.00
16.00
17.00
18.00
19.00
20.00

Old Habit >	New Habit >	New Actions >	New Affirmation / Mantra

My goals for the next week

Weekly Planner

My mantra for this week is ....

4 Major Goals I'm Focused On This Week

1.　　　　　2.　　　　　3.　　　　　4.

Projects & appointments for this week	Target date	Actions for this week	Target date

- monday
- tuesday
- wednesday
- thursday
- friday
- saturday
- sunday

ideas space

....

....

....

Today I accept that....

The things I AM grateful for in my life are...

Today, I would love to do these actions...

1.
2.
3.

Today I AM focusing on being...

I AM
I AM
I AM
I AM

What went well today?

What could I have handled differently today?

How can I open up to new ways of doing things?

What am I proud of about today?

date:

reminders

....

....

....

....

....

....

| | **M & V** meditation & visualisation | | **I** inspiration |
| | **E** exercise | | |

6.00
7.00
8.00
9.00
10.00
11.00
12.00
13.00
14.00
15.00
16.00
17.00
18.00
19.00
20.00

thoughts space

....
....
....

....
....
....
....
....
....
....
....
....

Today I AM going to create...

M & V
meditation & visualisation

I
inspiration

E
exercise
....

Gratitude is Wisdom...

- 6.00
- 7.00
- 8.00
- 9.00
- 10.00
- 11.00
- 12.00
- 13.00
- 14.00
- 15.00
- 16.00
- 17.00
- 18.00
- 19.00
- 20.00

Today, I feel inspired to do...

1.
2.
3.

I create my day with my thoughts, therefore...

I AM
I AM
I AM
I AM

What did I love about today?

In what area would I like to grow?

What would I like to let go of?

How did I show leadership today?

date:

fun space

....
....
....

Today I AM open to the possibility of...

What I love about my work is...

Today I AM inspired to take these actions...
1.
2.
3.

I have a winning mindset and...
I AM
I AM
I AM
I AM

What have I learned today?

How was my mindset today?

What new habit do I want to adopt into my life?

How did I give value today?

date:

reminders

....
....
....
....
....
....
....

☐ **M & V** meditation & visualisation   ☐ **I** inspiration
☐ **E** exercise   ☐ ....

6.00
7.00
8.00
9.00
10.00
11.00
12.00
13.00
14.00
15.00
16.00
17.00
18.00
19.00
20.00

genius space

....
....
....

Today, it would be fun to...

I AM so grateful for the simple things like...

What is the best course of action to take today?

1.
2.
3.

Today I AM creative and...

I AM
I AM
I AM
I AM

What was fantastic about today?

What skill can I develop further?

What new mindset do I want to adopt into my life?

What did I do really well today?

M & V meditation & visualisation
I inspiration
E exercise

- 6.00
- 7.00
- 8.00
- 9.00
- 10.00
- 11.00
- 12.00
- 13.00
- 14.00
- 15.00
- 16.00
- 17.00
- 18.00
- 19.00
- 20.00

date:

dream space

....
....
....

Today I would love....

Today I AM so grateful for...

My top 3 inspired actions for today are...

1.
2.
3.

My intentions for today are...

I AM
I AM
I AM
I AM

What was great about today?

What did I learn today?

After today, what behaviour do I want to upgrade?

What strengths did I use today?

date:

reminders

....
....
....
....
....
....
....

☐ **M & V** meditation & visualisation ☐ **I** inspiration
☐ **E** exercise ☐ ....

6.00
7.00
8.00
9.00
10.00
11.00
12.00
13.00
14.00
15.00
16.00
17.00
18.00
19.00
20.00

creative space

....
....
....

What if (insert possibility)....

Appreciation & Gratitude list...

Today, I AM most inspired to do these actions...

1.
2.
3.

The mindset I wish to create today is...

I AM
I AM
I AM
I AM

What did I enjoy about today?

What challenged me today that I can grow from?

What would I like to create instead?

What did I do really well today?

M & V meditation & visualisation
I inspiration
E exercise

Time	
6.00	
7.00	
8.00	
9.00	
10.00	
11.00	
12.00	
13.00	
14.00	
15.00	
16.00	
17.00	
18.00	
19.00	
20.00	

date:

My week in review

Weekly Check-in

What major goals have I achieved this month?

☐ Review Greatness Blueprint

☐ Review Purpose Statement

Where am I having success and why?

☐ Update 90 Day Planner

☐ Add Actions To Weekly Planner

☐ Plan Your Week

What are the biggest distractions in my life and how can I remove them?

8.00

9.00

What is one thing I can do next week that will create the biggest results in my life?

10.00

11.00

What am I committed to achieving in my life right now?

12.00

13.00

14.00

What is my home and work environment like? Does it inspire me?

15.00

16.00

GET SOME ALTITUDE Where is my current attitude on a scale from 1-10? How can I get some more altitude and upgrade my attitude?

17.00

18.00

What disempowering thoughts are holding me back and how can I upgrade those?

19.00

20.00

date:

| Old Habit > | New Habit > | New Actions > | New Affirmation / Mantra |

My goals for the next week

Weekly Planner

My mantra for this week is ....

4 Major Goals I'm Focused On This Week

| 1. | 2. | 3. | 4. |

| Projects & appointments for this week | Target date | Actions for this week | Target date |

monday

tuesday

wednesday

thursday

friday

saturday

sunday

dream space

....
....
....

Today I would love....

Today I AM so grateful for...

My top 3 inspired actions for today are...

1.
2.
3.

My intentions for today are...

I AM

I AM

I AM

I AM

What was great about today?

What did I learn today?

After today, what behaviour do I want to upgrade?

What strengths did I use today?

date:

reminders

....
....
....
....
....
....
....

■ **M & V** meditation & visualisation ■ **I** inspiration
■ **E** exercise ■ ....

6.00
7.00
8.00
9.00
10.00
11.00
12.00
13.00
14.00
15.00
16.00
17.00
18.00
19.00
20.00

creative space

....

....

....

What if (insert possibility)....

Appreciation & Gratitude list...

M & V
meditation & visualisation

I
inspiration

E
exercise

....

Today, I AM most inspired to do these actions...

1.
2.
3.

The mindset I wish to create today is...

I AM
I AM
I AM
I AM

6.00
7.00
8.00
9.00
10.00
11.00
12.00

What did I enjoy about today?

13.00
14.00
15.00

What challenged me today that I can grow from?

16.00
17.00

What would I like to create instead?

18.00
19.00

What did I do really well today?

20.00

date:

ideas space

....
....
....

Today I accept that....

The things I AM grateful for in my life are...

Today, I would love to do these actions...

1.
2.
3.

Today I AM focusing on being...

I AM
I AM
I AM
I AM

What went well today?

What could I have handled differently today?

How can I open up to new ways of doing things?

What am I proud of about today?

date:

reminders

....
....
....
....
....
....
....

☐ **M & V** meditation & visualisation   ☐ **I** inspiration
☐ **E** exercise

6.00
7.00
8.00
9.00
10.00
11.00
12.00
13.00
14.00
15.00
16.00
17.00
18.00
19.00
20.00

thoughts space

....
....
....

Today I AM going to create...

Gratitude is Wisdom...

M & V meditation & visualisation
I inspiration
E exercise

Today, I feel inspired to do...

1.
2.
3.

I create my day with my thoughts, therefore...

I AM
I AM
I AM
I AM

6.00
7.00
8.00
9.00
10.00
11.00

What did I love about today?

12.00
13.00
14.00

In what area would I like to grow?

15.00
16.00

What would I like to let go of?

17.00
18.00

How did I show leadership today?

19.00
20.00

date:

fun space

....
....
....

Today I AM open to the possibility of...

What I love about my work is...

Today I AM inspired to take these actions...

1.
2.
3.

I have a winning mindset and...

I AM
I AM
I AM
I AM

What have I learned today?

How was my mindset today?

What new habit do I want to adopt into my life?

How did I give value today?

date:

reminders

....
....
....
....
....
....
....
....

☐ **M & V** meditation & visualisation   ☐ **I** inspiration
☐ **E** exercise   ☐ ....

6.00
7.00
8.00
9.00
10.00
11.00
12.00
13.00
14.00
15.00
16.00
17.00
18.00
19.00
20.00

genius space

I AM open to receive

Today, it would be fun to...

I AM so grateful for the simple things like...

M & V
meditation & visualisation

I
inspiration

E
exercise

What is the best course of action to take today?

1.
2.
3.

Today I AM creative and...

I AM
I AM
I AM
I AM

What was fantastic about today?

What skill can I develop further?

What new mindset do I want to adopt into my life?

What did I do really well today?

6.00
7.00
8.00
9.00
10.00
11.00
12.00
13.00
14.00
15.00
16.00
17.00
18.00
19.00
20.00

date:

90 Day Check-in

Welcome to your 90-day check-in! It's time to celebrate your achievements, identify what needs attention, check your life balance, and set your focus for the next 90 days. Use the answers to the questions to plan your next quarter and adjust your goals, intentions, and actions accordingly. Transfer these to Your Achievements page to keep inspired and motivated about your progress.

What major goals have I completed this past 90 days?
What am I happy about?

How can I align more with my Greatness Blueprint and overall purpose? Does my vision still inspire me or do I need to upgrade my strategy?

What would I love to create in the next 90 days?
What goal or project am I focusing on?

What new mindset do I wish to develop?
What is no longer acceptable to me?

How do I feel about the 8 areas of my life?
How can I become more balanced and happy?
What areas of my life need attention?

Am I embracing change or resisting it?
How can I open up to more expansion?

Do I have a good team of people around me?
How can I surround myself with great people?
Who is my mentor?

What else have I noticed about my life in the last 90 days?

- ☐ Review Greatness Blueprint
- ☐ Review Purpose Statement
- ☐ Review Your Yearly Planner
- ☐ Complete Next 90 Day Planner
- ☐ Plan Your Week
- ☐ Celebrate Your Progress

My goals for the next 90 days

90 Day Planner

Goal:

Project:

Target date:

Actions to complete this goal:

1.
2.
3.
4.

Why I'd love to achieve this goal:

How will I feel when I've reached this goal?

Goal:

Project:

Target date:

Actions to complete this goal:

1.
2.
3.
4.

Why I'd love to achieve this goal:

How will I feel when I've reached this goal?

Goal:

Project:

Target date:

Actions to complete this goal:

1.
2.
3.
4.

Why I'd love to achieve this goal:

How will I feel when I've reached this goal?

Goal:

Project:

Target date:

Actions to complete this goal:

1.
2.
3.
4.

Why I'd love to achieve this goal:

How will I feel when I've reached this goal?

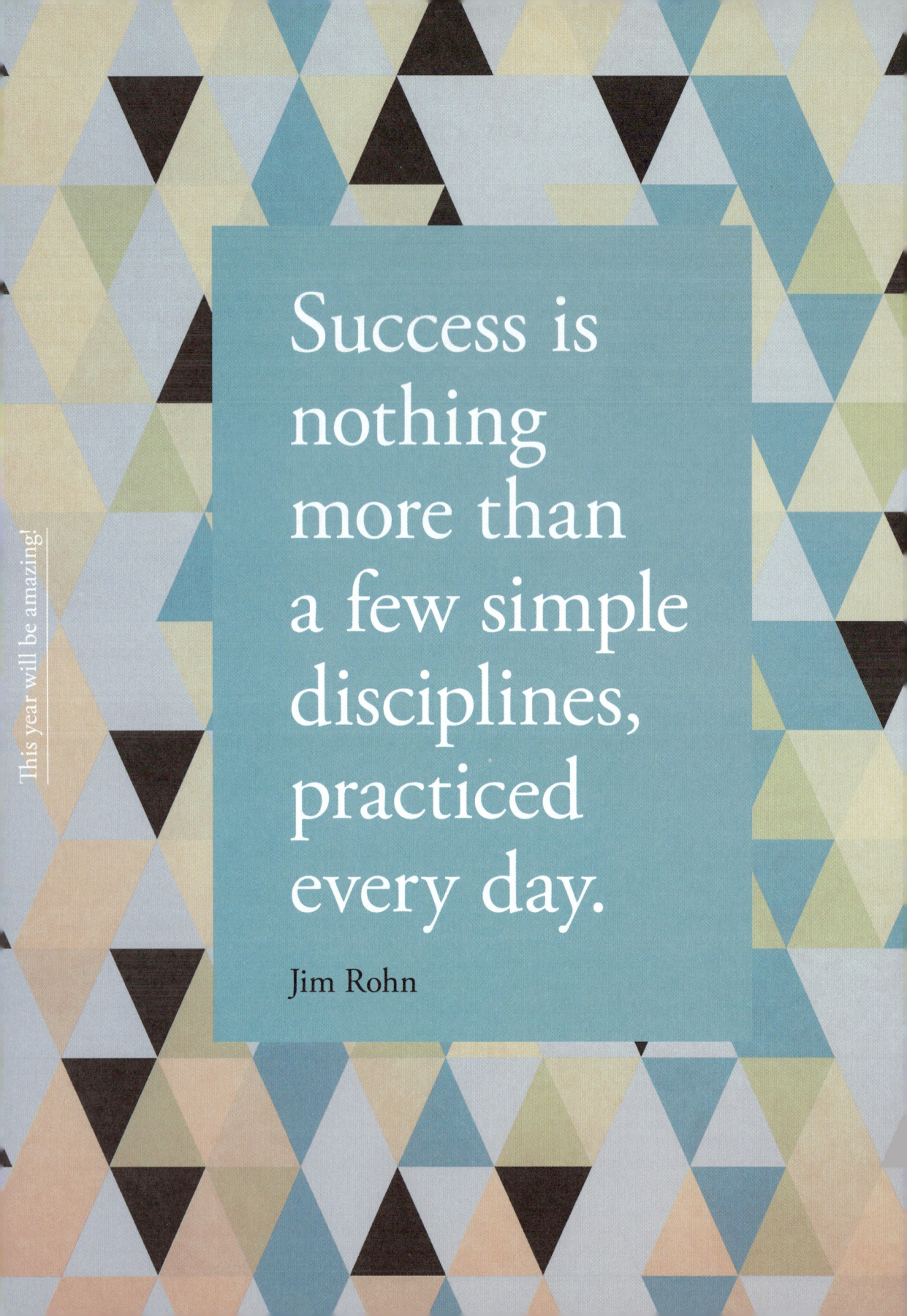

Success is nothing more than a few simple disciplines, practiced every day.

Jim Rohn

This year will be amazing!

My Genius Space

My goals for the next week

Weekly Planner

My mantra for this week is ....

4 Major Goals I'm Focused On This Week

1.	2.	3.	4.

Projects & appointments for this week	Target date	Actions for this week	Target date
monday			
tuesday			
wednesday			
thursday			
friday			
saturday			
sunday			

dream space

....

....

....

Today I would love....

Today I AM so grateful for...

My top 3 inspired actions for today are...

1.
2.
3.

My intentions for today are...

I AM

I AM

I AM

I AM

What was great about today?

What did I learn today?

After today, what behaviour do I want to upgrade?

What strengths did I use today?

date:

reminders

....

....

....

....

....

....

....

☐ **M & V** meditation & visualisation   ☐ **I** inspiration

☐ **E** exercise   ☐ ....

6.00
7.00
8.00
9.00
10.00
11.00
12.00
13.00
14.00
15.00
16.00
17.00
18.00
19.00
20.00

creative space

I AM wonderful

What if (insert possibility)....

Appreciation & Gratitude list...

M & V meditation & visualisation
I inspiration
E exercise

Today, I AM most inspired to do these actions...

1.
2.
3.

The mindset I wish to create today is...

I AM
I AM
I AM
I AM

What did I enjoy about today?

What challenged me today that I can grow from?

What would I like to create instead?

What did I do really well today?

6.00
7.00
8.00
9.00
10.00
11.00
12.00
13.00
14.00
15.00
16.00
17.00
18.00
19.00
20.00

date:

ideas space

....
....
....

Today I accept that....

The things I AM grateful for in my life are...

Today, I would love to do these actions...

1.
2.
3.

Today I AM focusing on being...

I AM
I AM
I AM
I AM

What went well today?

What could I have handled differently today?

How can I open up to new ways of doing things?

What am I proud of about today?

date:

reminders

....
....
....
....
....
....
....
....

☐ **M & V** meditation & visualisation   ☐ **I** inspiration
☐ **E** exercise   ☐ ....

6.00
7.00
8.00
9.00
10.00
11.00
12.00
13.00
14.00
15.00
16.00
17.00
18.00
19.00
20.00

thoughts space

....
....
....

Today I AM going to create...

Gratitude is Wisdom...

M & V	meditation & visualisation
I	inspiration
E	exercise

Today, I feel inspired to do...
1.
2.
3.

I create my day with my thoughts, therefore...
I AM
I AM
I AM
I AM

What did I love about today?

In what area would I like to grow?

What would I like to let go of?

How did I show leadership today?

6.00
7.00
8.00
9.00
10.00
11.00
12.00
13.00
14.00
15.00
16.00
17.00
18.00
19.00
20.00

date:

open space

....
....
....

Today I AM going to enjoy...

When I AM grateful I open up to more...

What would I do today, if it was my last?
1.
2.
3.

Today...
I AM
I AM
I AM
I AM

What was interesting about today?

What habit would I like to develop after today?

What beliefs would I like to upgrade?

What strengths did I use today?

date:

reminders

....
....
....
....
....
....
....

☐ **M & V** meditation & visualisation   ☐ **I** inspiration
☐ **E** exercise   ☐ ....

6.00
7.00
8.00
9.00
10.00
11.00
12.00
13.00
14.00
15.00
16.00
17.00
18.00
19.00
20.00

invention space

....
....
....

Today is my opportunity to...

Today, I give thanks for...

M & V
meditation & visualisation

I
inspiration

E
exercise ....

My inspired actions for today are...

1.
2.
3.

	6.00
	7.00
	8.00
	9.00
	10.00
	11.00
	12.00
	13.00
	14.00
	15.00
	16.00
	17.00
	18.00
	19.00
	20.00

Today I honor how I feel and...

I AM
I AM
I AM
I AM

What was fun about today?

What was today's lesson?

What new behaviour can I adopt into my life?

What did I succeed at...

date:

My week in review

Weekly Check-in

What projects have I completed this week?

☐ Review Greatness Blueprint

☐ Review Purpose Statement

What's going well and why is it?

☐ Update 90 Day Planner

☐ Add Actions To Weekly Planner

☐ Plan Your Week

What's most challenging and how can I turn it into an opportunity?

8.00

9.00

What is one thing I can do next week that will create the biggest results in my life?

10.00

11.00

12.00

What am I happy about right now?

13.00

14.00

How am I using my time? How can I prioritise better?

15.00

16.00

GET SOME ALTITUDE Where is my current attitude on a scale from 1-10? How can I get some more altitude and upgrade my attitude?

17.00

18.00

19.00

What fears are holding me back and how can I overcome those?

20.00

date:

Old Habit >	New Habit >	New Actions >	New Affirmation / Mantra

My goals for the next week

Weekly Planner

My mantra for this week is ....

4 Major Goals I'm Focused On This Week

| 1. | 2. | 3. | 4. |

| Projects & appointments for this week | Target date | Actions for this week | Target date |

- monday
- tuesday
- wednesday
- thursday
- friday
- saturday
- sunday

fun space

....
....
....

Today I AM open to the possibility of...

What I love about my work is...

Today I AM inspired to take these actions...

1.
2.
3.

I have a winning mindset and...

I AM
I AM
I AM
I AM

What have I learned today?

How was my mindset today?

What new habit do I want to adopt into my life?

How did I give value today?

date:

reminders

....
....
....
....
....
....
....

☐ **M & V** meditation & visualisation   ☐ **I** inspiration
☐ **E** exercise   ☐ ....

6.00
....
7.00
....
8.00
....
9.00
....
10.00
....
11.00
....
12.00
....
13.00
....
14.00
....
15.00
....
16.00
....
17.00
....
18.00
....
19.00
....
20.00
....

genius space

....
....
....

Today, it would be fun to...

I AM so grateful for the simple things like...

M & V meditation & visualisation
I inspiration
E exercise

What is the best course of action to take today?

1.
2.
3.

Today I AM creative and...

I AM
I AM
I AM
I AM

6.00
7.00
8.00
9.00
10.00
11.00
12.00

What was fantastic about today?

13.00
14.00

What skill can I develop further?

15.00
16.00

What new mindset do I want to adopt into my life?

17.00
18.00

What did I do really well today?

19.00
20.00

date:

dream space

....
....
....

Today I would love....

Today I AM so grateful for...

My top 3 inspired actions for today are...

1.
2.
3.

My intentions for today are...

I AM
I AM
I AM
I AM

What was great about today?

What did I learn today?

After today, what behaviour do I want to upgrade?

What strengths did I use today?

date:

reminders

....
....
....
....
....
....
....

☐ **M & V** meditation & visualisation ☐ **I** inspiration
☐ **E** exercise ☐ ....

6.00
7.00
8.00
9.00
10.00
11.00
12.00
13.00
14.00
15.00
16.00
17.00
18.00
19.00
20.00

creative space

....
....
....

I AM focused

What if (insert possibility)....

Appreciation & Gratitude list...

Today, I AM most inspired to do these actions...

1.
2.
3.

The mindset I wish to create today is...

I AM
I AM
I AM
I AM

What did I enjoy about today?

What challenged me today that I can grow from?

What would I like to create instead?

What did I do really well today?

M & V meditation & visualisation
I inspiration
E exercise

- 6.00
- 7.00
- 8.00
- 9.00
- 10.00
- 11.00
- 12.00
- 13.00
- 14.00
- 15.00
- 16.00
- 17.00
- 18.00
- 19.00
- 20.00

date:

ideas space

....
....
....

Today I accept that....

The things I AM grateful for in my life are...

Today, I would love to do these actions...

1.
2.
3.

Today I AM focusing on being...

I AM
I AM
I AM
I AM

What went well today?

What could I have handled differently today?

How can I open up to new ways of doing things?

What am I proud of about today?

date:

reminders

....
....
....
....
....
....
....

☐ **M & V** meditation & visualisation   ☐ **I** inspiration
☐ **E** exercise   ☐ ....

6.00
7.00
8.00
9.00
10.00
11.00
12.00
13.00
14.00
15.00
16.00
17.00
18.00
19.00
20.00

thoughts space

....
....
....

Today I AM going to create...

Gratitude is Wisdom...

M & V meditation & visualisation ☐ **I** inspiration

E exercise ☐ ....

Today, I feel inspired to do...

1.
2.
3.

I create my day with my thoughts, therefore...

I AM
I AM
I AM
I AM

What did I love about today?

In what area would I like to grow?

What would I like to let go of?

How did I show leadership today?

6.00
7.00
8.00
9.00
10.00
11.00
12.00
13.00
14.00
15.00
16.00
17.00
18.00
19.00
20.00

date:

My week in review

Weekly Check-in

What projects have I completed this week?

☐ Review Greatness Blueprint

☐ Review Purpose Statement

What's going well and why is it?

☐ Update 90 Day Planner

☐ Add Actions To Weekly Planner

☐ Plan Your Week

What's most challenging and how can I turn it into an opportunity?

8.00

9.00

What is one thing I can do next week that will create the biggest results in my life?

10.00

11.00

What am I happy about right now?

12.00

13.00

14.00

How am I using my time? How can I prioritise better?

15.00

16.00

GET SOME ALTITUDE Where is my current attitude on a scale from 1-10? How can I get some more altitude and upgrade my attitude?

17.00

18.00

19.00

What fears are holding me back and how can I overcome those?

20.00

date:

| Old Habit > | New Habit > | New Actions > | New Affirmation / Mantra |

My goals for the next week

Weekly Planner

My mantra for this week is ....

4 Major Goals I'm Focused On This Week

| 1. | 2. | 3. | 4. |

| Projects & appointments for this week | Target date | Actions for this week | Target date |

monday

tuesday

wednesday

thursday

friday

saturday

sunday

open space

....
....
....

Today I AM going to enjoy...

When I AM grateful I open up to more...

What would I do today, if it was my last?

1.
2.
3.

Today...
I AM
I AM
I AM
I AM

What was interesting about today?

What habit would I like to develop after today?

What beliefs would I like to upgrade?

What strengths did I use today?

date:

reminders

....
....
....
....
....
....
....

☐ **M & V** meditation & visualisation   ☐ **I** inspiration
☐ **E** exercise   ☐ ....

I AM focused

6.00
7.00
8.00
9.00
10.00
11.00
12.00
13.00
14.00
15.00
16.00
17.00
18.00
19.00
20.00

invention space

....
....
....

Today is my opportunity to...

Today, I give thanks for...

☐ **M & V** meditation & visualisation
☐ **I** inspiration
☐ **E** exercise
....

My inspired actions for today are...

1.
2.
3.

6.00
7.00
8.00
9.00
10.00
11.00

Today I honor how I feel and...

I AM
I AM
I AM
I AM

12.00
13.00
14.00

What was fun about today?

What was today's lesson?

15.00
16.00
17.00
18.00

What new behaviour can I adopt into my life?

19.00
20.00

What did I succeed at...

date:

fun space

....
....
....

Today I AM open to the possibility of...

What I love about my work is...

Today I AM inspired to take these actions...

1.
2.
3.

I have a winning mindset and...

I AM
I AM
I AM
I AM

What have I learned today?

How was my mindset today?

What new habit do I want to adopt into my life?

How did I give value today?

date:

reminders

....
....
....
....
....
....
....
....

☐ **M & V** meditation & visualisation   ☐ **I** inspiration
☐ **E** exercise   ☐ ....

6.00
7.00
8.00
9.00
10.00
11.00
12.00
13.00
14.00
15.00
16.00
17.00
18.00
19.00
20.00

genius space

....
....
....

Today, it would be fun to...

I AM so grateful for the simple things like...

What is the best course of action to take today?

1.
2.
3.

Today I AM creative and...

I AM
I AM
I AM
I AM

What was fantastic about today?

What skill can I develop further?

What new mindset do I want to adopt into my life?

What did I do really well today?

M & V meditation & visualisation
I inspiration
E exercise

- 6.00
- 7.00
- 8.00
- 9.00
- 10.00
- 11.00
- 12.00
- 13.00
- 14.00
- 15.00
- 16.00
- 17.00
- 18.00
- 19.00
- 20.00

date:

dream space

....
....
....

Today I would love....

Today I AM so grateful for...

My top 3 inspired actions for today are...

1.
2.
3.

My intentions for today are...

I AM
I AM
I AM
I AM

What was great about today?

What did I learn today?

After today, what behaviour do I want to upgrade?

What strengths did I use today?

date:

reminders

....
....
....
....
....
....
....

☐ **M & V** meditation & visualisation ☐ **I** inspiration
☐ **E** exercise ☐ ....

6.00
7.00
8.00
9.00
10.00
11.00
12.00
13.00
14.00
15.00
16.00
17.00
18.00
19.00
20.00

creative space

....
....
....

What if (insert possibility)....

Appreciation & Gratitude list...

M & V meditation & visualisation
I inspiration
E exercise

Today, I AM most inspired to do these actions...

1.
2.
3.

The mindset I wish to create today is...

I AM
I AM
I AM
I AM

What did I enjoy about today?

What challenged me today that I can grow from?

What would I like to create instead?

What did I do really well today?

6.00
7.00
8.00
9.00
10.00
11.00
12.00
13.00
14.00
15.00
16.00
17.00
18.00
19.00
20.00

date:

My week in review

Weekly Check-in

What have I achieved on my greatness blueprint this week?

☐ Review Greatness Blueprint

☐ Review Purpose Statement

Where am I seeing the desired results & why?

☐ Update 90 Day Planner

☐ Add Actions To Weekly Planner

☐ Plan Your Week

What do I need to start or stop?

What is one thing I can do next week that will create the biggest results in my life?

Where can I be a better leader?

Do I need to upgrade my communication skills? How can I be better?

GET SOME ALTITUDE Where is my current attitude on a scale from 1 -10? How can I get some more altitude and upgrade my attitude?

What negative attitudes are holding me back and how can I overcome those?

date:

| 8.00 |
| 9.00 |
| 10.00 |
| 11.00 |
| 12.00 |
| 13.00 |
| 14.00 |
| 15.00 |
| 16.00 |
| 17.00 |
| 18.00 |
| 19.00 |
| 20.00 |

| Old Habit > | New Habit > | New Actions > | New Affirmation / Mantra |

My goals for the next week

Weekly Planner

My mantra for this week is ....

4 Major Goals I'm Focused On This Week

1.
2.
3.
4.

Projects & appointments for this week	Target date	Actions for this week	Target date

monday

tuesday

wednesday

thursday

friday

saturday

sunday

ideas space

....
....
....

Today I accept that....

The things I AM grateful for in my life are...

Today, I would love to do these actions...

1.
2.
3.

Today I AM focusing on being...

I AM
I AM
I AM
I AM

What went well today?

What could I have handled differently today?

How can I open up to new ways of doing things?

What am I proud of about today?

date:

reminders

....
....
....
....
....
....
....

☐ **M & V** meditation & visualisation   ☐ **I** inspiration
☐ **E** exercise

6.00
7.00
8.00
9.00
10.00
11.00
12.00
13.00
14.00
15.00
16.00
17.00
18.00
19.00
20.00

thoughts space

....

....

....

Today I AM going to create...

Gratitude is Wisdom...

M & V
meditation & visualisation

I
inspiration

E
exercise

Today, I feel inspired to do...

1.
2.
3.

I create my day with my thoughts, therefore...

I AM
I AM
I AM
I AM

What did I love about today?

In what area would I like to grow?

What would I like to let go of?

How did I show leadership today?

6.00
7.00
8.00
9.00
10.00
11.00
12.00
13.00
14.00
15.00
16.00
17.00
18.00
19.00
20.00

date:

open space

....
....
....

Today I AM going to enjoy...

When I AM grateful I open up to more...

What would I do today, if it was my last?

1.
2.
3.

Today...

I AM
I AM
I AM
I AM

What was interesting about today?

What habit would I like to develop after today?

What beliefs would I like to upgrade?

What strengths did I use today?

date:

reminders

....
....
....
....
....
....
....

☐ **M & V** meditation & visualisation ☐ **I** inspiration
☐ **E** exercise ☐ ....

6.00
7.00
8.00
9.00
10.00
11.00
12.00
13.00
14.00
15.00
16.00
17.00
18.00
19.00
20.00

I AM *focused*

invention space

....
....
....

Today is my opportunity to...

Today, I give thanks for...

M & V meditation & visualisation
I inspiration
E exercise

My inspired actions for today are...

1.
2.
3.

6.00
7.00
8.00
9.00
10.00
11.00

Today I honor how I feel and...

I AM
I AM
I AM
I AM

12.00
13.00

What was fun about today?

14.00
15.00
16.00

What was today's lesson?

17.00

What new behaviour can I adopt into my life?

18.00
19.00
20.00

What did I succeed at...

date:

fun space

....
....
....

Today I AM open to the possibility of...

What I love about my work is...

Today I AM inspired to take these actions...

1.
2.
3.

I have a winning mindset and...

I AM
I AM
I AM
I AM

What have I learned today?

How was my mindset today?

What new habit do I want to adopt into my life?

How did I give value today?

date:

reminders

....
....
....
....
....
....

☐ **M & V** meditation & visualisation   ☐ **I** inspiration
☐ **E** exercise   ☐ ....

6.00
7.00
8.00
9.00
10.00
11.00
12.00
13.00
14.00
15.00
16.00
17.00
18.00
19.00
20.00

genius space

....
....
....

....
....
....
....

Today, it would be fun to...

....
....
....
....
....
....

I AM so grateful for the simple things like...

M & V
meditation & visualisation

I
inspiration

E
exercise

....

What is the best course of action to take today?

1.
2.
3.

6.00
7.00
8.00

Today I AM creative and...

9.00

I AM

I AM

10.00

I AM

I AM

11.00

12.00

What was fantastic about today?

13.00

14.00

What skill can I develop further?

15.00

16.00

What new mindset do I want to adopt into my life?

17.00

18.00

19.00

What did I do really well today?

20.00

date:

My week in review

Weekly Check-in

What major goals have I achieved this month?

☐ Review Greatness Blueprint

☐ Review Purpose Statement

Where am I having success and why?

☐ Update 90 Day Planner

☐ Add Actions To Weekly Planner

☐ Plan Your Week

What are the biggest distractions in my life and how can I remove them?

What is one thing I can do next week that will create the biggest results in my life?

What am I committed to achieving in my life right now?

What is my home and work environment like? Does it inspire me?

GET SOME ALTITUDE Where is my current attitude on a scale from 1-10? How can I get some more altitude and upgrade my attitude?

What disempowering thoughts are holding me back and how can I upgrade those?

date:

8.00
9.00
10.00
11.00
12.00
13.00
14.00
15.00
16.00
17.00
18.00
19.00
20.00

Old Habit >	New Habit >	New Actions >	New Affirmation / Mantra

My goals for the next week

Weekly Planner

My mantra for this week is ....

4 Major Goals I'm Focused On This Week

| 1. | 2. | 3. | 4. |

Projects & appointments for this week	Target date	Actions for this week	Target date
monday			
tuesday			
wednesday			
thursday			
friday			
saturday			
sunday			

dream space

....
....
....

Today I would love....

Today I AM so grateful for...

My top 3 inspired actions for today are...

1.
2.
3.

My intentions for today are...

I AM
I AM
I AM
I AM

date:

What was great about today?

What did I learn today?

After today, what behaviour do I want to upgrade?

What strengths did I use today?

reminders

....
....
....
....
....
....
....

☐ **M & V** meditation & visualisation ☐ **I** inspiration
☐ **E** exercise ☐ ....

6.00
....
7.00
....
8.00
....
9.00
....
10.00
....
11.00
....
12.00
....
13.00
....
14.00
....
15.00
....
16.00
....
17.00
....
18.00
....
19.00
....
20.00
....

creative space

....
....
....

What if (insert possibility)....

Appreciation & Gratitude list...

I AM wonderful

M & V meditation & visualisation   ☐ **I** inspiration

E exercise   ☐ ....

Today, I AM most inspired to do these actions...

1.
2.
3.

The mindset I wish to create today is...

I AM
I AM
I AM
I AM

What did I enjoy about today?

What challenged me today that I can grow from?

What would I like to create instead?

What did I do really well today?

6.00
7.00
8.00
9.00
10.00
11.00
12.00
13.00
14.00
15.00
16.00
17.00
18.00
19.00
20.00

date:

ideas space

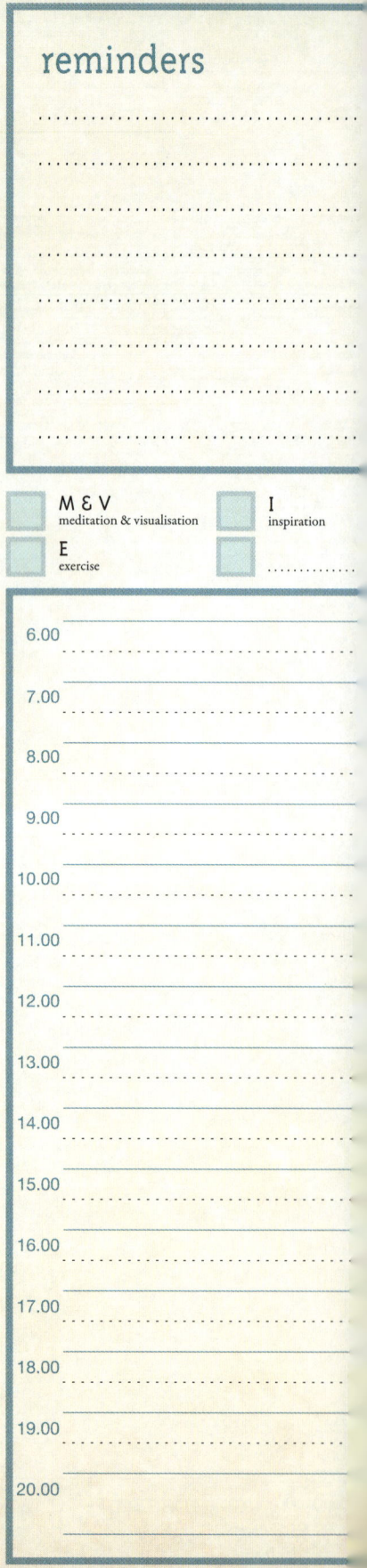

....

....

....

Today I accept that....

The things I AM grateful for in my life are...

Today, I would love to do these actions...

1.
2.
3.

Today I AM focusing on being...

I AM

I AM

I AM

I AM

What went well today?

What could I have handled differently today?

How can I open up to new ways of doing things?

What am I proud of about today?

date:

reminders

....
....
....
....
....
....
....

☐ **M & V** meditation & visualisation ☐ **I** inspiration
☐ **E** exercise ☐ ....

6.00
7.00
8.00
9.00
10.00
11.00
12.00
13.00
14.00
15.00
16.00
17.00
18.00
19.00
20.00

thoughts space

....
....
....

Today I AM going to create...

Gratitude is Wisdom...

M & V meditation & visualisation
I inspiration
E exercise
....

Today, I feel inspired to do...

1.
2.
3.

I create my day with my thoughts, therefore...

I AM
I AM
I AM
I AM

What did I love about today?

In what area would I like to grow?

What would I like to let go of?

How did I show leadership today?

6.00
7.00
8.00
9.00
10.00
11.00
12.00
13.00
14.00
15.00
16.00
17.00
18.00
19.00
20.00

date:

open space

....
....
....

Today I AM going to enjoy...

When I AM grateful I open up to more...

What would I do today, if it was my last?

1.
2.
3.

Today...

I AM
I AM
I AM
I AM

What was interesting about today?

What habit would I like to develop after today?

What beliefs would I like to upgrade?

What strengths did I use today?

date:

reminders

....
....
....
....
....
....
....

☐ **M & V** meditation & visualisation   ☐ **I** inspiration
☐ **E** exercise

6.00
7.00
8.00
9.00
10.00
11.00
12.00
13.00
14.00
15.00
16.00
17.00
18.00
19.00
20.00

invention space

....
....
....

Today is my opportunity to...

Today, I give thanks for...

M & V
meditation & visualisation

I
inspiration

E
exercise

My inspired actions for today are...

1.
2.
3.

6.00
7.00
8.00

Today I honor how I feel and...

I AM
I AM
I AM
I AM

9.00
10.00
11.00
12.00

What was fun about today?

13.00
14.00

What was today's lesson?

15.00
16.00

What new behaviour can I adopt into my life?

17.00
18.00

What did I succeed at...

19.00
20.00

date:

My week in review

Weekly Check-in

What projects have I completed this week?

☐ Review Greatness Blueprint

☐ Review Purpose Statement

What's going well and why is it?

☐ Update 90 Day Planner

☐ Add Actions To Weekly Planner

☐ Plan Your Week

What's most challenging and how can I turn it into an opportunity?

8.00

9.00

What is one thing I can do next week that will create the biggest results in my life?

10.00

11.00

12.00

What am I happy about right now?

13.00

14.00

How am I using my time? How can I prioritise better?

15.00

16.00

GET SOME ALTITUDE Where is my current attitude on a scale from 1-10? How can I get some more altitude and upgrade my attitude?

17.00

18.00

19.00

What fears are holding me back and how can I overcome those?

20.00

date:

| Old Habit > | New Habit > | New Actions > | New Affirmation / Mantra |

My goals for the next week

Weekly Planner

My mantra for this week is ....

4 Major Goals I'm Focused On This Week

| 1. | 2. | 3. | 4. |

Projects & appointments for this week	Target date	Actions for this week	Target date
monday			
tuesday			
wednesday			
thursday			
friday			
saturday			
sunday			

fun space

....
....
....

Today I AM open to the possibility of...

What I love about my work is...

Today I AM inspired to take these actions...

1.
2.
3.

I have a winning mindset and...

I AM
I AM
I AM
I AM

What have I learned today?

How was my mindset today?

What new habit do I want to adopt into my life?

How did I give value today?

date:

reminders

....
....
....
....
....
....
....

☐ **M & V** meditation & visualisation ☐ **I** inspiration
☐ **E** exercise ☐ ....

6.00
7.00
8.00
9.00
10.00
11.00
12.00
13.00
14.00
15.00
16.00
17.00
18.00
19.00
20.00

genius space

....
....
....

Today, it would be fun to...

I AM so grateful for the simple things like...

What is the best course of action to take today?

1.
2.
3.

Today I AM creative and...

I AM
I AM
I AM
I AM

What was fantastic about today?

What skill can I develop further?

What new mindset do I want to adopt into my life?

What did I do really well today?

☐ **M & V** meditation & visualisation
☐ **I** inspiration
☐ **E** exercise
....

6.00
7.00
8.00
9.00
10.00
11.00
12.00
13.00
14.00
15.00
16.00
17.00
18.00
19.00
20.00

date:

dream space

....
....
....

Today I would love....

Today I AM so grateful for...

My top 3 inspired actions for today are...

1.
2.
3.

My intentions for today are...

I AM
I AM
I AM
I AM

What was great about today?

What did I learn today?

After today, what behaviour do I want to upgrade?

What strengths did I use today?

date:

reminders

....
....
....
....
....
....
....

☐ **M & V** meditation & visualisation ☐ **I** inspiration
☐ **E** exercise ☐ ....

6.00
7.00
8.00
9.00
10.00
11.00
12.00
13.00
14.00
15.00
16.00
17.00
18.00
19.00
20.00

creative space

....

....

....

What if (insert possibility)....

Appreciation & Gratitude list...

M & V
meditation & visualisation

I
inspiration

E
exercise

Today, I AM most inspired to do these actions...

1.
2.
3.

The mindset I wish to create today is...

I AM

I AM

I AM

I AM

6.00
7.00
8.00
9.00
10.00
11.00
12.00 — What did I enjoy about today?
13.00
14.00
15.00 — What challenged me today that I can grow from?
16.00
17.00 — What would I like to create instead?
18.00
19.00 — What did I do really well today?
20.00

I AM focused

date:

ideas space

....
....
....

Today I accept that....

The things I AM grateful for in my life are...

Today, I would love to do these actions...

1.
2.
3.

Today I AM focusing on being...

I AM
I AM
I AM
I AM

What went well today?

What could I have handled differently today?

How can I open up to new ways of doing things?

What am I proud of about today?

date:

reminders

....
....
....
....
....
....
....

☐ **M & V** meditation & visualisation   ☐ **I** inspiration
☐ **E** exercise   ☐ ....

6.00
7.00
8.00
9.00
10.00
11.00
12.00
13.00
14.00
15.00
16.00
17.00
18.00
19.00
20.00

thoughts space

....
....
....

Today I AM going to create...

Gratitude is Wisdom...

M & V meditation & visualisation
I inspiration
E exercise

Today, I feel inspired to do...

1.
2.
3.

I create my day with my thoughts, therefore...

I AM
I AM
I AM
I AM

What did I love about today?

In what area would I like to grow?

What would I like to let go of?

How did I show leadership today?

6.00
7.00
8.00
9.00
10.00
11.00
12.00
13.00
14.00
15.00
16.00
17.00
18.00
19.00
20.00

date:

My week in review

Weekly Check-in

What projects have I completed this week?

☐ Review Greatness Blueprint

☐ Review Purpose Statement

What's going well and why is it?

☐ Update 90 Day Planner

☐ Add Actions To Weekly Planner

☐ Plan Your Week

What's most challenging and how can I turn it into an opportunity?

8.00

9.00

What is one thing I can do next week that will create the biggest results in my life?

10.00

11.00

What am I happy about right now?

12.00

13.00

14.00

How am I using my time? How can I prioritise better?

15.00

16.00

GET SOME ALTITUDE Where is my current attitude on a scale from 1-10? How can I get some more altitude and upgrade my attitude?

17.00

18.00

19.00

What fears are holding me back and how can I overcome those?

20.00

date:

| Old Habit > | New Habit > | New Actions > | New Affirmation / Mantra |

My goals for the next week

Weekly Planner

My mantra for this week is ....

4 Major Goals I'm Focused On This Week

| 1. | 2. | 3. | 4. |

| Projects & appointments for this week | Target date | Actions for this week | Target date |

- monday
- tuesday
- wednesday
- thursday
- friday
- saturday
- sunday

open space

....
....
....

Today I AM going to enjoy...

When I AM grateful I open up to more...

What would I do today, if it was my last?

1.
2.
3.

Today...

I AM
I AM
I AM
I AM

What was interesting about today?

What habit would I like to develop after today?

What beliefs would I like to upgrade?

What strengths did I use today?

date:

reminders

....
....
....
....
....
....
....
....

☐ **M & V** meditation & visualisation   ☐ **I** inspiration
☐ **E** exercise   ☐ ....

6.00
7.00
8.00
9.00
10.00
11.00
12.00
13.00
14.00
15.00
16.00
17.00
18.00
19.00
20.00

invention space

....
....
....

Today is my opportunity to...

Today, I give thanks for...

My inspired actions for today are...

1.
2.
3.

Today I honor how I feel and...

I AM
I AM
I AM
I AM

What was fun about today?

What was today's lesson?

What new behaviour can I adopt into my life?

What did I succeed at...

M & V
meditation & visualisation

I
inspiration

E
exercise

6.00
7.00
8.00
9.00
10.00
11.00
12.00
13.00
14.00
15.00
16.00
17.00
18.00
19.00
20.00

date:

fun space

....
....
....

Today I AM open to the possibility of...

I AM focused

What I love about my work is...

Today I AM inspired to take these actions...

1.
2.
3.

I have a winning mindset and...

I AM
I AM
I AM
I AM

What have I learned today?

How was my mindset today?

What new habit do I want to adopt into my life?

How did I give value today?

date:

reminders

....
....
....
....
....
....
....

☐ **M & V** meditation & visualisation   ☐ **I** inspiration
☐ **E** exercise   ☐ ....

Time	
6.00	
7.00	
8.00	
9.00	
10.00	
11.00	
12.00	
13.00	
14.00	
15.00	
16.00	
17.00	
18.00	
19.00	
20.00	

genius space

....
....

Today, it would be fun to...

I AM so grateful for the simple things like...

What is the best course of action to take today?

1.
2.
3.

Today I AM creative and...

I AM
I AM
I AM
I AM

What was fantastic about today?

What skill can I develop further?

What new mindset do I want to adopt into my life?

What did I do really well today?

M & V meditation & visualisation
I inspiration
E exercise

6.00
7.00
8.00
9.00
10.00
11.00
12.00
13.00
14.00
15.00
16.00
17.00
18.00
19.00
20.00

date:

dream space

....
....
....

Today I would love....

Today I AM so grateful for...

My top 3 inspired actions for today are...

1.
2.
3.

My intentions for today are...

I AM
I AM
I AM
I AM

What was great about today?

What did I learn today?

After today, what behaviour do I want to upgrade?

What strengths did I use today?

date:

reminders

....
....
....
....
....
....
....
....

☐ **M & V** meditation & visualisation ☐ **I** inspiration
☐ **E** exercise ☐ ....

6.00
7.00
8.00
9.00
10.00
11.00
12.00
13.00
14.00
15.00
16.00
17.00
18.00
19.00
20.00

creative space

....
....
....

What if (insert possibility)....

Appreciation & Gratitude list...

☐ **M & V** meditation & visualisation   ☐ **I** inspiration
☐ **E** exercise   ☐ ....

Today, I AM most inspired to do these actions...

1.
2.
3.

The mindset I wish to create today is...

I AM
I AM
I AM
I AM

What did I enjoy about today?

What challenged me today that I can grow from?

What would I like to create instead?

What did I do really well today?

....
....
....
....
....
....
....

.... 6.00
.... 7.00
.... 8.00
.... 9.00
.... 10.00
.... 11.00
.... 12.00
.... 13.00
.... 14.00
.... 15.00
.... 16.00
.... 17.00
.... 18.00
.... 19.00
.... 20.00

date:

My week in review

Weekly Check-in

What have I achieved on my greatness blueprint this week?

☐ Review Greatness Blueprint

☐ Review Purpose Statement

Where am I seeing the desired results & why?

☐ Update 90 Day Planner

☐ Add Actions To Weekly Planner

☐ Plan Your Week

What do I need to start or stop?

What is one thing I can do next week that will create the biggest results in my life?

Where can I be a better leader?

Do I need to upgrade my communication skills? How can I be better?

GET SOME ALTITUDE Where is my current attitude on a scale from 1-10? How can I get some more altitude and upgrade my attitude?

What negative attitudes are holding me back and how can I overcome those?

date:

8.00
9.00
10.00
11.00
12.00
13.00
14.00
15.00
16.00
17.00
18.00
19.00
20.00

| Old Habit > | New Habit > | New Actions > | New Affirmation / Mantra |

My goals for the next week

Weekly Planner

My mantra for this week is ....

4 Major Goals I'm Focused On This Week

| 1. | 2. | 3. | 4. |

Projects & appointments for this week	Target date	Actions for this week	Target date
monday			
tuesday			
wednesday			
thursday			
friday			
saturday			
sunday			

ideas space

....
....
....

Today I accept that....

The things I AM grateful for in my life are...

Today, I would love to do these actions...

1.
2.
3.

Today I AM focusing on being...

I AM
I AM
I AM
I AM

What went well today?

What could I have handled differently today?

How can I open up to new ways of doing things?

What am I proud of about today?

date:

reminders

....
....
....
....
....
....

☐ **M & V** meditation & visualisation   ☐ **I** inspiration
☐ **E** exercise   ☐ ....

6.00
7.00
8.00
9.00
10.00
11.00
12.00
13.00
14.00
15.00
16.00
17.00
18.00
19.00
20.00

thoughts space

....
....
....

Today I AM going to create...

Gratitude is Wisdom...

M & V meditation & visualisation
I inspiration
E exercise

Today, I feel inspired to do...

1.
2.
3.

I create my day with my thoughts, therefore...

I AM
I AM
I AM
I AM

What did I love about today?

In what area would I like to grow?

What would I like to let go of?

How did I show leadership today?

6.00
7.00
8.00
9.00
10.00
11.00
12.00
13.00
14.00
15.00
16.00
17.00
18.00
19.00
20.00

date:

open space

....

....

....

Today I AM going to enjoy...

When I AM grateful I open up to more...

What would I do today, if it was my last?

1.
2.
3.

Today...

I AM
I AM
I AM
I AM

What was interesting about today?

What habit would I like to develop after today?

What beliefs would I like to upgrade?

What strengths did I use today?

date:

reminders

....
....
....
....
....
....
....

☐ **M & V** meditation & visualisation   ☐ **I** inspiration
☐ **E** exercise   ☐ ....

6.00
7.00
8.00
9.00
10.00
11.00
12.00
13.00
14.00
15.00
16.00
17.00
18.00
19.00
20.00

invention space

....
....
....

Today is my opportunity to...

Today, I give thanks for...

I AM focused

M & V		I	
meditation & visualisation		inspiration	
E			
exercise			....

My inspired actions for today are...

1.
2.
3.

6.00
7.00
8.00

Today I honor how I feel and...

9.00

I AM
I AM

10.00

I AM
I AM

11.00

12.00

What was fun about today?

13.00

14.00

What was today's lesson?

15.00

16.00

What new behaviour can I adopt into my life?

17.00

18.00

19.00

What did I succeed at...

20.00

date:

fun space

....
....
....

Today I AM open to the possibility of...

What I love about my work is...

Today I AM inspired to take these actions...

1.
2.
3.

I have a winning mindset and...

I AM
I AM
I AM
I AM

What have I learned today?

How was my mindset today?

What new habit do I want to adopt into my life?

How did I give value today?

date:

reminders

....
....
....
....
....
....
....
....

☐ **M & V** meditation & visualisation   ☐ **I** inspiration
☐ **E** exercise   ☐ ....

6.00 ....
7.00 ....
8.00 ....
9.00 ....
10.00 ....
11.00 ....
12.00 ....
13.00 ....
14.00 ....
15.00 ....
16.00 ....
17.00 ....
18.00 ....
19.00 ....
20.00 ....

genius space

....
....
....

Today, it would be fun to...

I AM so grateful for the simple things like...

☐ **M & V** meditation & visualisation ☐ **I** inspiration
☐ **E** exercise ☐ ....

What is the best course of action to take today?

1.
2.
3.

Today I AM creative and...

I AM
I AM
I AM
I AM

What was fantastic about today?

What skill can I develop further?

What new mindset do I want to adopt into my life?

What did I do really well today?

date:

6.00
7.00
8.00
9.00
10.00
11.00
12.00
13.00
14.00
15.00
16.00
17.00
18.00
19.00
20.00

My week in review

Weekly Check-in

What major goals have I achieved this month?

☐ Review Greatness Blueprint

☐ Review Purpose Statement

Where am I having success and why?

☐ Update 90 Day Planner

☐ Add Actions To Weekly Planner

☐ Plan Your Week

What are the biggest distractions in my life and how can I remove them?

8.00

9.00

What is one thing I can do next week that will create the biggest results in my life?

10.00

11.00

What am I committed to achieving in my life right now?

12.00

13.00

14.00

What is my home and work environment like? Does it inspire me?

15.00

16.00

GET SOME ALTITUDE Where is my current attitude on a scale from 1-10? How can I get some more altitude and upgrade my attitude?

17.00

18.00

19.00

What disempowering thoughts are holding me back and how can I upgrade those?

20.00

date:

Old Habit >   New Habit >   New Actions >   New Affirmation / Mantra

My goals for the next week

Weekly Planner

My mantra for this week is ....

4 Major Goals I'm Focused On This Week

1.	2.	3.	4.

Projects & appointments for this week	Target date	Actions for this week	Target date
monday			
tuesday			
wednesday			
thursday			
friday			
saturday			
sunday			

dream space

....
....
....

Today I would love....

Today I AM so grateful for...

My top 3 inspired actions for today are...

1.
2.
3.

My intentions for today are...

I AM

I AM

I AM

I AM

What was great about today?

What did I learn today?

After today, what behaviour do I want to upgrade?

What strengths did I use today?

date:

reminders

....
....
....
....
....
....
....
....

☐ **M & V** meditation & visualisation   ☐ **I** inspiration
☐ **E** exercise   ☐ ....

6.00
7.00
8.00
9.00
10.00
11.00
12.00
13.00
14.00
15.00
16.00
17.00
18.00
19.00
20.00

creative space

....
....
....

What if (insert possibility)....

I AM wonderful

Appreciation & Gratitude list...

M & V meditation & visualisation
I inspiration
E exercise

Today, I AM most inspired to do these actions...

1.
2.
3.

	6.00
	7.00
	8.00
	9.00
	10.00
	11.00
	12.00
	13.00
	14.00
	15.00
	16.00
	17.00
	18.00
	19.00
	20.00

The mindset I wish to create today is...

I AM
I AM
I AM
I AM

What did I enjoy about today?

What challenged me today that I can grow from?

What would I like to create instead?

What did I do really well today?

date:

ideas space

....
....
....

Today I accept that....

The things I AM grateful for in my life are...

Today, I would love to do these actions...

1.
2.
3.

Today I AM focusing on being...

I AM
I AM
I AM
I AM

What went well today?

What could I have handled differently today?

How can I open up to new ways of doing things?

What am I proud of about today?

date:

reminders

....
....
....
....
....
....
....
....

☐ **M & V** meditation & visualisation   ☐ **I** inspiration
☐ **E** exercise   ☐ ....

6.00
7.00
8.00
9.00
10.00
11.00
12.00
13.00
14.00
15.00
16.00
17.00
18.00
19.00
20.00

thoughts space

....
....
....

Today I AM going to create...

Gratitude is Wisdom...

Today, I feel inspired to do...

1.
2.
3.

I create my day with my thoughts, therefore...

I AM
I AM
I AM
I AM

What did I love about today?

In what area would I like to grow?

What would I like to let go of?

How did I show leadership today?

M & V meditation & visualisation
I inspiration
E exercise

- 6.00
- 7.00
- 8.00
- 9.00
- 10.00
- 11.00
- 12.00
- 13.00
- 14.00
- 15.00
- 16.00
- 17.00
- 18.00
- 19.00
- 20.00

date:

open space

....
....
....

Today I AM going to enjoy...

When I AM grateful I open up to more...

What would I do today, if it was my last?

1.
2.
3.

Today...

I AM
I AM
I AM
I AM

What was interesting about today?

What habit would I like to develop after today?

What beliefs would I like to upgrade?

What strengths did I use today?

date:

reminders

....
....
....
....
....
....
....

☐ **M & V** meditation & visualisation   ☐ **I** inspiration
☐ **E** exercise   ☐ ....

6.00
7.00
8.00
9.00
10.00
11.00
12.00
13.00
14.00
15.00
16.00
17.00
18.00
19.00
20.00

invention space

....
....
....

Today is my opportunity to...

Today, I give thanks for...

M & V meditation & visualisation
I inspiration
E exercise
....

My inspired actions for today are...

1.
2.
3.

6.00
7.00
8.00

Today I honor how I feel and...

I AM
I AM
I AM
I AM

9.00
10.00
11.00
12.00

What was fun about today?

13.00
14.00

What was today's lesson?

15.00
16.00

What new behaviour can I adopt into my life?

17.00
18.00
19.00

What did I succeed at...

20.00

date:

My week in review

Weekly Check-in

What projects have I completed this week?

☐ Review Greatness Blueprint

☐ Review Purpose Statement

☐ Update 90 Day Planner

What's going well and why is it?

☐ Add Actions To Weekly Planner

☐ Plan Your Week

What's most challenging and how can I turn it into an opportunity?

What is one thing I can do next week that will create the biggest results in my life?

What am I happy about right now?

How am I using my time? How can I prioritise better?

GET SOME ALTITUDE Where is my current attitude on a scale from 1-10? How can I get some more altitude and upgrade my attitude?

What fears are holding me back and how can I overcome those?

date:

8.00
9.00
10.00
11.00
12.00
13.00
14.00
15.00
16.00
17.00
18.00
19.00
20.00

Old Habit >	New Habit >	New Actions >	New Affirmation / Mantra

My goals for the next week

Weekly Planner

My mantra for this week is ....

4 Major Goals I'm Focused On This Week

1.	2.	3.	4.

Projects & appointments for this week	Target date	Actions for this week	Target date
monday			
tuesday			
wednesday			
thursday			
friday			
saturday			
sunday			

fun space

....
....
....

Today I AM open to the possibility of...

What I love about my work is...

Today I AM inspired to take these actions...
1.
2.
3.

I have a winning mindset and...

I AM
I AM
I AM
I AM

What have I learned today?

How was my mindset today?

What new habit do I want to adopt into my life?

How did I give value today?

date:

reminders

....
....
....
....
....
....

☐ **M & V** meditation & visualisation   ☐ **I** inspiration
☐ **E** exercise   ☐ ....

6.00
7.00
8.00
9.00
10.00
11.00
12.00
13.00
14.00
15.00
16.00
17.00
18.00
19.00
20.00

… genius space

………………………………………………………………………
………………………………………………………………………
………………………………………………………………………

Today, it would be fun to...

I AM so grateful for the simple things like...

M & V meditation & visualisation
I inspiration
E exercise

What is the best course of action to take today?

1.
2.
3.

Today I AM creative and...

I AM
I AM
I AM
I AM

What was fantastic about today?

What skill can I develop further?

What new mindset do I want to adopt into my life?

What did I do really well today?

6.00
7.00
8.00
9.00
10.00
11.00
12.00
13.00
14.00
15.00
16.00
17.00
18.00
19.00
20.00

date:

dream space

....
....
....

Today I would love....

Today I AM so grateful for...

My top 3 inspired actions for today are...

1.
2.
3.

My intentions for today are...

I AM
I AM
I AM
I AM

What was great about today?

What did I learn today?

After today, what behaviour do I want to upgrade?

What strengths did I use today?

date:

reminders

....
....
....
....
....
....
....

☐ **M & V** meditation & visualisation ☐ **I** inspiration
☐ **E** exercise ☐ ....

6.00
7.00
8.00
9.00
10.00
11.00
12.00
13.00
14.00
15.00
16.00
17.00
18.00
19.00
20.00

I AM focused

creative space

....
....
....

What if (insert possibility)....

Appreciation & Gratitude list...

M & V meditation & visualisation
I inspiration
E exercise

Today, I AM most inspired to do these actions...

1.
2.
3.

The mindset I wish to create today is...

I AM
I AM
I AM
I AM

6.00	
7.00	
8.00	
9.00	
10.00	
11.00	
12.00	What did I enjoy about today?
13.00	
14.00	
15.00	What challenged me today that I can grow from?
16.00	
17.00	What would I like to create instead?
18.00	
19.00	What did I do really well today?
20.00	

date:

ideas space

....
....
....

Today I accept that....

The things I AM grateful for in my life are...

Today, I would love to do these actions...

1.
2.
3.

Today I AM focusing on being...

I AM
I AM
I AM
I AM

What went well today?

What could I have handled differently today?

How can I open up to new ways of doing things?

What am I proud of about today?

date:

reminders

....
....
....
....
....
....
....

☐ **M & V** meditation & visualisation   ☐ **I** inspiration
☐ **E** exercise   ☐ ....

6.00
7.00
8.00
9.00
10.00
11.00
12.00
13.00
14.00
15.00
16.00
17.00
18.00
19.00
20.00

thoughts space

....
....
....

Today I AM going to create...

....
....
....
....
....
....
....

Gratitude is Wisdom...

M & V
meditation & visualisation

I
inspiration

E
exercise ....

Today, I feel inspired to do...

1.
2.
3.

.... 6.00
.... 7.00
.... 8.00

I create my day with my thoughts, therefore...

I AM
I AM
I AM
I AM

.... 9.00
.... 10.00
.... 11.00
.... 12.00

What did I love about today?

.... 13.00
.... 14.00

In what area would I like to grow?

.... 15.00
.... 16.00
.... 17.00

What would I like to let go of?

.... 18.00
.... 19.00

How did I show leadership today?

.... 20.00

date:

My week in review

Weekly Check-in

date:

What projects have I completed this week?

What's going well and why is it?

What's most challenging and how can I turn it into an opportunity?

What is one thing I can do next week that will create the biggest results in my life?

What am I happy about right now?

How am I using my time? How can I prioritise better?

GET SOME ALTITUDE Where is my current attitude on a scale from 1-10? How can I get some more altitude and upgrade my attitude?

What fears are holding me back and how can I overcome those?

- [ ] Review Greatness Blueprint
- [ ] Review Purpose Statement
- [ ] Update 90 Day Planner
- [ ] Add Actions To Weekly Planner
- [ ] Plan Your Week

8.00
9.00
10.00
11.00
12.00
13.00
14.00
15.00
16.00
17.00
18.00
19.00
20.00

Old Habit >	New Habit >	New Actions >	New Affirmation / Mantra

My goals for the next week

Weekly Planner

My mantra for this week is ....

4 Major Goals I'm Focused On This Week

| 1. | 2. | 3. | 4. |

| Projects & appointments for this week | Target date | Actions for this week | Target date |

monday

tuesday

wednesday

thursday

friday

saturday

sunday

open space

....
....
....

Today I AM going to enjoy...

When I AM grateful I open up to more...

What would I do today, if it was my last?
1.
2.
3.

Today...
I AM
I AM
I AM
I AM

What was interesting about today?

What habit would I like to develop after today?

What beliefs would I like to upgrade?

What strengths did I use today?

date:

reminders

....
....
....
....
....
....
....

☐ **M & V** meditation & visualisation   ☐ **I** inspiration
☐ **E** exercise   ☐ ....

6.00
7.00
8.00
9.00
10.00
11.00
12.00
13.00
14.00
15.00
16.00
17.00
18.00
19.00
20.00

invention space

....
....
....
....
....
....
....
....

Today is my opportunity to...

Today, I give thanks for...

☐ M & V meditation & visualisation
☐ I inspiration
☐ E exercise
☐ ....

My inspired actions for today are...

1.
2.
3.

6.00
7.00
8.00
9.00
10.00
11.00

Today I honor how I feel and...

I AM
I AM
I AM
I AM

12.00
13.00
14.00

What was fun about today?

What was today's lesson?

15.00
16.00
17.00
18.00

What new behaviour can I adopt into my life?

19.00

What did I succeed at...

20.00

date:

fun space

....
....
....

Today I AM open to the possibility of...

What I love about my work is...

Today I AM inspired to take these actions...
1.
2.
3.

I have a winning mindset and...
I AM
I AM
I AM
I AM

What have I learned today?

How was my mindset today?

What new habit do I want to adopt into my life?

How did I give value today?

date:

reminders

....
....
....
....
....
....
....

☐ **M & V** meditation & visualisation   ☐ **I** inspiration
☐ **E** exercise   ☐ ....

6.00
7.00
8.00
9.00
10.00
11.00
12.00
13.00
14.00
15.00
16.00
17.00
18.00
19.00
20.00

genius space

Today, it would be fun to...

I AM focused

I AM so grateful for the simple things like...

M & V
meditation & visualisation

I
inspiration

E
exercise

What is the best course of action to take today?

1.
2.
3.

6.00
7.00
8.00
9.00
10.00
11.00

Today I AM creative and...

I AM
I AM
I AM
I AM

12.00
13.00

What was fantastic about today?

14.00
15.00

What skill can I develop further?

16.00
17.00

What new mindset do I want to adopt into my life?

18.00
19.00

What did I do really well today?

20.00

date:

dream space

....

....

....

Today I would love....

Today I AM so grateful for...

My top 3 inspired actions for today are...

1.
2.
3.

My intentions for today are...

I AM

I AM

I AM

I AM

What was great about today?

What did I learn today?

After today, what behaviour do I want to upgrade?

What strengths did I use today?

date:

reminders

....

....

....

....

....

....

....

☐ **M & V** meditation & visualisation   ☐ **I** inspiration
☐ **E** exercise   ☐ ....

6.00
7.00
8.00
9.00
10.00
11.00
12.00
13.00
14.00
15.00
16.00
17.00
18.00
19.00
20.00

creative space

....
....
....

What if (insert possibility)....

Appreciation & Gratitude list...

☐ **M & V**
  meditation & visualisation   ☐ **I**
  inspiration

☐ **E**
  exercise   ☐ ....

Today, I AM most inspired to do these actions...

1.
2.
3.

The mindset I wish to create today is...

I AM
I AM
I AM
I AM

What did I enjoy about today?

What challenged me today that I can grow from?

What would I like to create instead?

What did I do really well today?

6.00
7.00
8.00
9.00
10.00
11.00
12.00
13.00
14.00
15.00
16.00
17.00
18.00
19.00
20.00

date:

My week in review

Weekly Check-in

What have I achieved on my greatness blueprint this week?

☐ Review Greatness Blueprint

☐ Review Purpose Statement

Where am I seeing the desired results & why?

☐ Update 90 Day Planner

☐ Add Actions To Weekly Planner

☐ Plan Your Week

What do I need to start or stop?

```
8.00
_____
9.00
_____
10.00
_____
11.00
_____
12.00
_____
13.00
_____
14.00
_____
15.00
_____
16.00
_____
17.00
_____
18.00
_____
19.00
_____
20.00
```

What is one thing I can do next week that will create the biggest results in my life?

Where can I be a better leader?

date:

Do I need to upgrade my communication skills? How can I be better?

GET SOME ALTITUDE Where is my current attitude on a scale from 1-10? How can I get some more altitude and upgrade my attitude?

What negative attitudes are holding me back and how can I overcome those?

| Old Habit > | New Habit > | New Actions > | New Affirmation / Mantra |

My goals for the next week

Weekly Planner

My mantra for this week is ....

4 Major Goals I'm Focused On This Week

| 1. | 2. | 3. | 4. |

| Projects & appointments for this week | Target date | Actions for this week | Target date |

monday

tuesday

wednesday

thursday

friday

saturday

sunday

ideas space

....

....

....

Today I accept that....

The things I AM grateful for in my life are...

Today, I would love to do these actions...

1.
2.
3.

Today I AM focusing on being...

I AM

I AM

I AM

I AM

What went well today?

What could I have handled differently today?

How can I open up to new ways of doing things?

What am I proud of about today?

date:

reminders

....

....

....

....

....

....

....

☐ **M & V** meditation & visualisation ☐ **I** inspiration

☐ **E** exercise ☐ ....

6.00
....
7.00
....
8.00
....
9.00
....
10.00
....
11.00
....
12.00
....
13.00
....
14.00
....
15.00
....
16.00
....
17.00
....
18.00
....
19.00
....
20.00
....

thoughts space

....

....

....

Today I AM going to create...

Gratitude is Wisdom...

□ **M & V** meditation & visualisation
□ **I** inspiration
□ **E** exercise
□ ....

Today, I feel inspired to do...

1.
2.
3.

I create my day with my thoughts, therefore...

I AM
I AM
I AM
I AM

— 6.00
— 7.00
— 8.00
— 9.00
— 10.00
— 11.00
— 12.00

What did I love about today?

— 13.00
— 14.00
— 15.00

In what area would I like to grow?

— 16.00
— 17.00

What would I like to let go of?

— 18.00
— 19.00

How did I show leadership today?

— 20.00

date:

open space

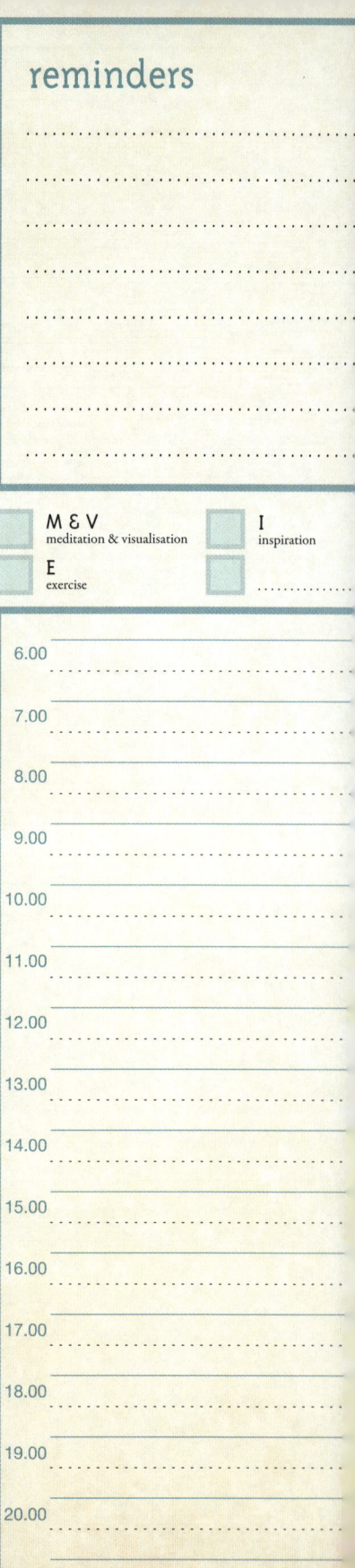

....
....
....

Today I AM going to enjoy...

When I AM grateful I open up to more...

What would I do today, if it was my last?

1.
2.
3.

Today...

I AM
I AM
I AM
I AM

What was interesting about today?

What habit would I like to develop after today?

What beliefs would I like to upgrade?

What strengths did I use today?

date:

reminders

....
....
....
....
....
....
....

☐ **M & V** meditation & visualisation ☐ **I** inspiration
☐ **E** exercise ☐ ....

6.00
7.00
8.00
9.00
10.00
11.00
12.00
13.00
14.00
15.00
16.00
17.00
18.00
19.00
20.00

invention space

....
....
....

Today is my opportunity to...

Today, I give thanks for...

M & V meditation & visualisation
I inspiration
E exercise

My inspired actions for today are...

1.
2.
3.

6.00	
7.00	
8.00	Today I honor how I feel and...
9.00	I AM
	I AM
10.00	I AM
	I AM
11.00	
12.00	What was fun about today?
13.00	
14.00	What was today's lesson?
15.00	
16.00	
17.00	What new behaviour can I adopt into my life?
18.00	
19.00	What did I succeed at...
20.00	

date:

fun space

....
....
....

Today I AM open to the possibility of...

What I love about my work is...

Today I AM inspired to take these actions...

1.
2.
3.

I have a winning mindset and...

I AM
I AM
I AM
I AM

What have I learned today?

How was my mindset today?

What new habit do I want to adopt into my life?

How did I give value today?

date:

reminders

....
....
....
....
....
....
....

☐ **M & V** meditation & visualisation ☐ **I** inspiration
☐ **E** exercise ☐ ....

6.00
7.00
8.00
9.00
10.00
11.00
12.00
13.00
14.00
15.00
16.00
17.00
18.00
19.00
20.00

genius space

....
....
....

Today, it would be fun to...

I AM so grateful for the simple things like...

M & V meditation & visualisation	**I** inspiration
E exercise	....

What is the best course of action to take today?

1.
2.
3.

6.00
7.00
8.00   Today I AM creative and...
9.00   I AM
              I AM
10.00   I AM
              I AM
11.00

12.00   What was fantastic about today?
13.00
14.00
15.00   What skill can I develop further?
16.00
17.00   What new mindset do I want to adopt into my life?
18.00
19.00   What did I do really well today?
20.00

date:

My week in review

Weekly Check-in

What major goals have I achieved this month?

☐ Review Greatness Blueprint

☐ Review Purpose Statement

Where am I having success and why?

☐ Update 90 Day Planner

☐ Add Actions To Weekly Planner

☐ Plan Your Week

What are the biggest distractions in my life and how can I remove them?

8.00

9.00

What is one thing I can do next week that will create the biggest results in my life?

10.00

11.00

12.00

What am I committed to achieving in my life right now?

13.00

14.00

What is my home and work environment like? Does it inspire me?

15.00

16.00

GET SOME ALTITUDE Where is my current attitude on a scale from 1-10? How can I get some more altitude and upgrade my attitude?

17.00

18.00

19.00

What disempowering thoughts are holding me back and how can I upgrade those?

20.00

date:

| Old Habit > | New Habit > | New Actions > | New Affirmation / Mantra |

My goals for the next week

Weekly Planner

My mantra for this week is ....

4 Major Goals I'm Focused On This Week

| 1. | 2. | 3. | 4. |

| Projects & appointments for this week | Target date | Actions for this week | Target date |

monday

tuesday

wednesday

thursday

friday

saturday

sunday

dream space

....
....
....

Today I would love....

Today I AM so grateful for...

My top 3 inspired actions for today are...

1.
2.
3.

My intentions for today are...

I AM
I AM
I AM
I AM

What was great about today?

What did I learn today?

After today, what behaviour do I want to upgrade?

What strengths did I use today?

date:

reminders

....
....
....
....
....
....
....

☐ **M & V** meditation & visualisation   ☐ **I** inspiration
☐ **E** exercise   ☐ ....

6.00	
7.00	
8.00	
9.00	
10.00	
11.00	
12.00	
13.00	
14.00	
15.00	
16.00	
17.00	
18.00	
19.00	
20.00	

creative space

....
....
....

What if (insert possibility)....

Appreciation & Gratitude list...

□ M & V meditation & visualisation
□ I inspiration
□ E exercise
□ ....

Today, I AM most inspired to do these actions...

1.
2.
3.

The mindset I wish to create today is...

I AM
I AM
I AM
I AM

6.00
7.00
8.00
9.00
10.00
11.00
12.00

What did I enjoy about today?

13.00
14.00

What challenged me today that I can grow from?

15.00
16.00

What would I like to create instead?

17.00
18.00

19.00

What did I do really well today?

20.00

date:

ideas space

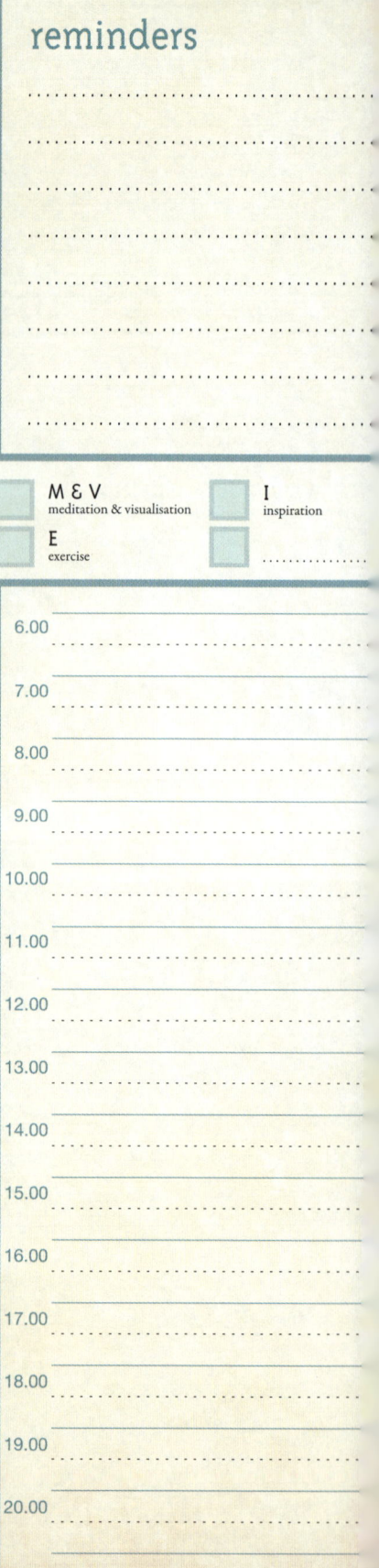

....
....
....

Today I accept that....

The things I AM grateful for in my life are...

Today, I would love to do these actions...

1.
2.
3.

Today I AM focusing on being...

I AM
I AM
I AM
I AM

What went well today?

What could I have handled differently today?

How can I open up to new ways of doing things?

What am I proud of about today?

date:

reminders

....
....
....
....
....
....
....

☐ **M & V** meditation & visualisation ☐ **I** inspiration
☐ **E** exercise ☐ ....

6.00
7.00
8.00
9.00
10.00
11.00
12.00
13.00
14.00
15.00
16.00
17.00
18.00
19.00
20.00

thoughts space

....
....
                                                      ....

.... Today I AM going to create...
....
....
.... Gratitude is Wisdom...
....

☐ **M & V** meditation & visualisation   ☐ **I** inspiration
☐ **E** exercise   ☐ ....

Today, I feel inspired to do...

1.
2.
3.

Time	
6.00	
7.00	
8.00	
9.00	
10.00	
11.00	
12.00	
13.00	
14.00	
15.00	
16.00	
17.00	
18.00	
19.00	
20.00	

I create my day with my thoughts, therefore...

I AM
I AM
I AM
I AM

What did I love about today?

In what area would I like to grow?

What would I like to let go of?

How did I show leadership today?

date:

open space

....
....
....

Today I AM going to enjoy...

I AM focused

When I AM grateful I open up to more...

What would I do today, if it was my last?

1.
2.
3.

Today...

I AM
I AM
I AM
I AM

What was interesting about today?

What habit would I like to develop after today?

What beliefs would I like to upgrade?

What strengths did I use today?

date:

reminders

....
....
....
....
....
....
....
....

☐ **M & V** meditation & visualisation   ☐ **I** inspiration
☐ **E** exercise   ☐ ....

6.00
7.00
8.00
9.00
10.00
11.00
12.00
13.00
14.00
15.00
16.00
17.00
18.00
19.00
20.00

invention space

....

....

....

Today is my opportunity to...

Today, I give thanks for...

☐ M & V
meditation & visualisation

☐ I
inspiration

☐ E
exercise

....

My inspired actions for today are...

1.
2.
3.

Today I honor how I feel and...

I AM
I AM
I AM
I AM

What was fun about today?

What was today's lesson?

What new behaviour can I adopt into my life?

What did I succeed at...

6.00
7.00
8.00
9.00
10.00
11.00
12.00
13.00
14.00
15.00
16.00
17.00
18.00
19.00
20.00

date:

Yearly Review

If you've made it to this point in the journal, it's likely you've gone through an incredible personal transformation. Congratulations on your amazing commitment, discipline and focus. Now it's time to reflect back over your year and note your achievements, your lessons, your challenges and your breakthroughs, and celebrate how far you've come!

Use these observations as stepping-stones to catapult you into another year of greatness.

Help us to spread our transformational journals by sharing your images using #dailygreatnessjournal on social media or review the Dailygreatness Journal on our website or on Amazon and go in our monthly draw to win a free copy!

To reorder your Dailygreatness Journal and browse all our other journals, online courses and content, visit dailygreatnessjournal.com

▶ Review Your Greatness Blueprint

▶ Review Your Purpose Statement

▶ Review Your Yearly Planner

▶ Start dreaming a new dream and vision

What major goals have I achieved?

How has my mindset improved?

In what ways has my life changed for the better?

What have I learned about myself?

What have I learned about my relationships?

How am I better embracing change?

What new positive habits have I adopted?

What challenges have I faced and overcome?

What breakthroughs have I had?

What do I need to let go of before moving forward into another year?

What areas of personal growth would I like to focus on for next year?

What major goals would I like to achieve next year?

Appendix i

Get into a comfortable position. You may like to sit in a comfortable chair, or cross-legged on the floor. You want to be able to completely relax while staying alert. Close your eyes and begin to focus on your breath. As you inhale and exhale, focus on the rise and fall of your belly, or the tip of your nose. Begin to clear you mind with each new breath. The idea is to stay unattached to your thoughts and as they arise (which they will) just let them go without continuing to think anymore about them. Think of your thoughts as clouds and as they float into your mind, just let them drift right on by and keep letting go. Focus instead on your breath, and soon the quiet space in between your thoughts will become longer. As you practice this technique, you will naturally progress to being able to meditate for longer periods, so start with 10-15 minutes and over time aim to progress to 30 minutes.

Appendix ii

1. Know yourself. You must know what your beliefs are, both conscious and unconscious, to fully understand what is creating your reality.
2. Make your goal of value to others or for your highest good.
3. Visualise your goal with as much detail and emotion as possible. See it clearly in your mind and feel the emotions it evokes in your body.
4. Focus only on the end result. Don't try to figure out how it is going to come to you.
5. Let it go.
6. Take action. Go about your business and continue to stay alert for any signs, synchronicities and assistance from the universe.

Appendix iii

The Life Revolution.

To check your life balance and current level of satisfaction in all eight areas of your life, begin by assessing how satisfied you are for each area on a scale of 0 (very dissatisfied) to 5 (very satisfied). Using a coloured pen, mark your score with a dot in the appropriate segment & corresponding number on the circle. Do this for each area, and then join the dots with the same coloured pen. How does it look? How satisfied are you? Is your circle in balance? Now, it's time to consider your 'ideal' level for each area. With a different coloured pen, mark your 'ideal' scores around the circle and again, join the dots. Now you should have a clear picture of your current life balance.

Where are the gaps? What areas would you like to upgrade? These are the areas in which to direct your energy and focus to bring you back into balance and wholeness. There will always be areas that don't get as much attention as you'd like, but this tool will keep you aware, so you can continually re-balance and re-align. Identifying the things in your life that sap your energy and life force will help you better direct your energy, and allow you to focus on activities that empower you. Once you have identified the main areas that need attention, it's time to make a plan of action. Challenge: Name one thing you can do in each area that will immediately improve your life. Make a commitment to these actions by adding them to your daily top 3 inspired actions and weekly planner.

Appendix iv

A 6-Step Process for creating and achieving meaningful goals:

1

What do you want? = Your Final Outcome

Set your goal – this is the biggest picture of what you want to be, do, or have in any area of your life. This is the final outcome and not a project or action towards something, but the ultimate goal you are shooting for. What would you love? What do you feel passionate about? What have you always wished for? What is deep within your heart waiting to be expressed?

2. Why do you want it? = Your Reason

Know why you want your goal. A strong 'why' is the motivation you need to propel you towards your goals. If you can't find a big enough why, you may need to re-evaluate if your goal is something you really want. A good question to ask is, "When I achieve this goal will I be happier and have more of what is important to me?"

3. Who do you need to BE? = Your Mindset

This step is all about the mindset behind the goal. If you want to be a successful leader, then you need to BE a leader and develop the mindset of what a good leader is. If you want to lose weight, then you need to BE a healthy person and develop the habits and mindset of a healthy person. If you want to make more money, then you need to BE someone who is wealthy and develop the mindset for wealth.

Once you start to step into BEing then you will DO the actions, and you will HAVE what you desire. It can't happen any other way. A starting place for creating the right mindset, is stating your intentions in I AM statements e.g. I AM a fantastic writer and author. I AM a healthy eater. I AM wealthy.

4. How will you get it? = Your Actions

Make a plan by breaking down your goals into projects. These could also be called milestones.

List all the actions it will take to complete the project.

Who do you need on your team? Make a list of all the people who will help you achieve your goals including mentors, coaches, friends, supporters, and other colleagues or business partners. If it works for you, share your goals with others to keep you accountable.

5. When will you have it? = Your Timeframe

Make a timeframe for when each action, project, and goal is to be achieved – being flexible to account for hold-ups and unforeseen challenges.

6. Which fears, obstacles, or limiting beliefs will you come up against? = Your Self - Awareness

Now is the time to be honest with yourself and get all your fears, limiting beliefs, and potential challenges out on the table. By recognising these, you can prepare yourself for when they arrive – and they will. You will see them for what they are, and by not giving them your power, you can keep moving past them. Fear is just a natural instinct that warns us that we are moving into unknown territory. This is a good sign, as all of our goals and dreams live outside our comfort zone. When you feel fear, it's a sign that you're getting closer to your goal.

Keep in mind, it's not the achievement of the goals that matters, but who you become through working towards them. Attachment to our goals pushes them away, while non-attachment allows the perfect experience to unfold for us when we are willing to let go and follow our inspiration.

When setting goals, you must consider all the dimensions of your life: body, mind, and spirit. To achieve sustainable goals, a change must occur on the inside, before you see the physical manifestation of it on the outside. All change starts within, and all goals are achieved through your inner self-belief.

Without expanding your consciousness through self-awareness practices, major goals are very hard to achieve. If you do achieve them, without having built a solid foundation, you will not be able to sustain them. i.e.: you might make a lot of money, but then you will soon lose it; you might begin to lose a lot of weight on a diet, but eventually you put it all back on; you might get a great opportunity, but you will sabotage it. To achieve any goal in any area of your life, an inner transformation has to take place first. When this happens, the outer condition transforms itself almost effortlessly. What are your goals, and are they coming from your mind or your heart?